TRANSFORM YOUR SPEAKING SKILLS

Transform Your Speaking Skills
Copyright © 2022 by Will Greenblatt.
All rights reserved.

Published by Grammar Factory Publishing, an imprint of MacMillan Company
Limited.

Grammar Factory Publishing
MacMillan Company Limited
25 Telegram Mews, 39th Floor, Suite 3906
Toronto, Ontario, Canada
M5V 3Z1

www.grammarfactory.com

Greenblatt, Will
Transform Your Speaking Skills: Gain Confidence, Captivate Audiences and Advance
    Your Career / Will Greenblatt.

Paperback ISBN 978-1-98973-780-4
eBook ISBN 978-1-98973-781-1

    1. LAN026000 LANGUAGE ARTS & DISCIPLINES / Public Speaking & Speech
Writing. 2. BUS059000 BUSINESS & ECONOMICS / Skills. 3. BUS107000 BUSINESS
& ECONOMICS / Personal Success.

Production Credits
Cover design by Designerbility
Interior layout design by Dania Zafar
Book production and editorial services by Grammar Factory Publishing

Grammar Factory's Carbon Neutral Publishing Commitment
Grammar Factory Publishing is proud to be neutralizing the carbon footprint of all
printed copies of its authors' books printed by or ordered directly through Grammar
Factory or its affiliated companies through the purchase of Gold Standard-Certified
International Offsets.

Disclaimer
The material in this publication is of the nature of general comment only and does
not represent professional advice. It is not intended to provide specific guidance for
particular circumstances, and it should not be relied on as the basis for any decision
to take action or not take action on any matter which it covers. Readers should
obtain professional advice where appropriate, before making any such decision. To
the maximum extent permitted by law, the author and publisher disclaim all respon-
sibility and liability to any person, arising directly or indirectly from any person taking
or not taking action based on the information in this publication.

TRANSFORM YOUR SPEAKING SKILLS

Gain confidence, captivate audiences,
and advance your career

WILL GREENBLATT

TESTIMONIALS

"*Transform Your Speaking Skills* is an indispensable, must-read guide to what many entrepreneurs fear most — public speaking. Will Greenblatt paints a compelling picture of why speaking skills are so important, and then clearly lays out how to develop your own communication and public speaking skill set. This book is unique; it's not solely focused on the act of standing up on stage in front of a large crowd. Greenblatt recognizes — and helps readers recognize — that speaking in public comes in many forms, and improving your abilities in this area will have a profound, positive impact on your life, both professional and personal."

Scott A. MacMillan, content strategist, best-selling author of *Entrepreneur to Author*, and host of the *Entrepreneur to Author Podcast*

"Will Greenblatt has taken the work I've seen him and his team do time and time again, coaching founders to deliver pitches that raise millions in VC funding... and translated it into a practical, easy to read, emotionally engaging and valuable book. A must-read for anyone looking to level up their public speaking."

Tariq Haddadin, Program Manager, TechStars Toronto

"I watched Will transform a group of forty-plus entrepreneurs at an event I hired him for. Everyone loved it and got so much out of it... This book uses the concepts he taught us that day and takes a deep dive into each one... highly recommended."

Peter Petrik, Technology Expert, Entrepreneur and Global Business Educator & Accelerator Facilitator @ Entrepreneurs' Organization

"In *Transform Your Speaking Skills*, Will Greenblatt has written a book that helps you get to the heart of your pitch and think about what really moves people; that can help you deliver your message in a way that really hits home, embracing vulnerability, using specific acting techniques, and using empathy to put yourself in your audience's shoes. I would recommend this book to anyone who wants to learn how to tell their story more powerfully."

Adrienne Palmer, CEO & Co-Founder, World Citizens Guide

Will is a great speaker who knows how to *captivate, inspire and motivate* people of all backgrounds to believe they can not only become great speakers, but leaders. I've had the opportunity to work with him directly and was encouraged as he used his fun personality, mixed with witty knowledge to depict the art of influencing through storytelling and how to speak with confidence. If you are ready to fight your fears... If you are ready to stand up on the stage of your life and thrive...If you are ready to get your message out of your head and into the world... If you are ready to get off the sidelines and begin sharing your greatness... It's time for you to step into your boldness! Pick up *Transform your Speaking Skills* today!

Amber Mabry, Co-Authour of Diamonds and Pearls: Affirmations of a Mompreneur Who Rocks

CONTENTS

Dedication

I'd like to dedicate this book to my mentors who helped get me here — especially Nicky, without whom this book would not exist — and my wife, Sarah, who helps me understand and care about life.

Foreword

I first heard Will speak in 2018 at an event for the fitness industry, where he was helping a group of about 100 gym owners and fitness instructors develop their public speaking skills. I was so impressed with Will's energy, passion, and ability to engage the audience that I could hardly wait for his talk to end so I could convince him to come to New Orleans the following week to coach a group of international professional facilitators.

This was the start of a streak of excellent sessions with Will, and since that time, I have worked with him on at least a dozen occasions. He has provided multiple group trainings and one-to-one coaching for spin instructors at Torq ride, a spin studio I've owned since 2016. He has led workshop modules for numerous clients through my brand strategy firm Parcel Design, and he has run "Train the Trainer" sessions for the Entrepreneurs Organization, an international non-profit with a membership of nearly 18,000 successful business owners around the world.

Will's candid style and improvisational trainings are incredibly versatile. His varied content is audience-specific and works for everyone, from those looking to speak English more clearly, to leaders and coaches looking for tips to manage difficult conversations, to those looking to improve their performance when speaking to a large group from a stage.

I have personally benefitted from Will's trainings, and keep in my back pocket his tips for improving my delivery, like the Speech Settings, "lower the stakes," and countless other game changers — most of which are covered in the pages ahead!

Enjoy this book — I can't think of anyone better to help you transform your speaking skills.

Julie Mitchell, serial entrepreneur, CEO @ Parcel Design,
and raving Will Greenblatt fan

Introduction

Speaking skills. Also known as: Stage presence. Social skills. Leadership. Oratorical prowess. Charisma. Animal magnetism?

It goes by many names, but we all know this quality when we see it in another human being. They speak, and we *listen*, eyebrows raised, leaning forward in our chairs, smiling slightly as we direct the most precious resource of the modern age toward them: our attention.

These people paint pictures with their words, tell powerful stories about themselves and other people, and make us feel like something *important* is happening and we're privileged to be witnessing it. And they are rewarded handsomely for it.

These confident communicators out-earn their peers, start successful business empires, and gain credibility, recognition and praise from their customers and colleagues. We all know this, but we assume that if we weren't born with *it*, we'll never have *it*. I certainly used to think so. And if you're like I was — and reading this book — chances are that on some level you believe that too. However, you may be curious and hoping to have your mind changed — thinking that if you *can* learn these skills, this book might help.

But before we answer the nature-versus-nurture question of how great speakers are made, it's worth asking: *why* is it that good communication skills allow some individuals to rise to the upper echelons of our society, even if they aren't (necessarily) as smart, hard-working, good-looking or otherwise advantaged as their peers?

The answer, at least in part, can be found by looking back thousands of years ago, to our days of hunting, gathering, and living in small tribes of around 150 people. During this time we were completely dependent on our fellow tribe members for survival (and they on us), but as individuals we needed to know certain things: Who could we trust? Who was a friend? Who was powerful? Who was dangerous? Who was sleeping with whom, and with whom might *we* be able to sleep (and thus pass on our genes)?

Good communication — effective speaking and listening — was key to answering these questions. If you noticed someone's clenched fists and furrowed eyebrows, and so responded in a soothing tone to avoid a fight, chances are you could avoid getting your head bashed in. Not only that, but those who were able to stand up around the campfire and *tell stories* to other members of the tribe — about where food, water, shelter and predatory animals could be found — provided tremendous value to their group, and were therefore given status and respect.

Both of these things — navigating complex social groups, and learning how to share life-saving information — had a profound impact on our evolution. Over time, communication became essential to our success as a species, leading us to create cities, nations, and even a global community connected by technology our ancestors could never have dreamed of. But today, despite how far we've come, many of our instincts remain based in evolutionary psychology. Although the stories we tell and the tribes we belong to have become much bigger and more sophisticated, those who communicate well with others — especially in groups — tend to rise above the rest of the tribe. You can see it in the way we deify actors and entertainers, or elect charismatic politicians, or hire candidates who are a better "culture fit" than their competitors, which simply means: "I like talking to them the best."

But back to our original question: can you *learn* how to communicate with confidence, clarity and conviction? Is the ability to move audiences with your presentations, gain recognition in your field, and become the empathetic leader you need to be within your grasp? The answer is absolutely *yes*, and this book is my effort to both convince you of that, and show you how.

You might identify as an introvert. You might be painfully shy. Speaking in front of more than three people might be a recurring nightmare of yours. Study after study lists public speaking as one of the biggest fears that people have. As Jerry Seinfeld has joked: "Many people would rather be lying in the casket than delivering the eulogy."

But I think the problem is deeper than just "glossophobia" (fear of public speaking). Almost every professional I've worked with suffers from some sort of negative self-image, which bubbles up when they have to talk to others about themselves or their work. Impostor syndrome, stage fright, freezing up — all of these simply mean *anxiety*, in one form or another.

Anxiety is another evolutionary gift from our hunter–gatherer ancestors. Those humans who weren't anxious and liked to relax would often get eaten; those who were satisfied with staying in the same territory might starve when the food ran out. All the people who survived pre-history were neurotic, paranoid, and self-doubting, and they passed those genes down to us (thanks, guys).

The great news is that, by tackling the issues of public speaking and communication, we can begin to peel back the layers of anxiety that stop us from doing so many other risky and rewarding things: starting a new business, asking for a raise, proposing, or starting therapy. I've had clients who have started dream jobs, dealt with painful buried memories, and grown wildly — not just as professionals, but as people — thanks in part to the process of self-discovery we went on together. My promise to you before we begin is that if you finish this book, you will gain the motivation and insight you need to really work on yourself, as well as a healthy dose of the compassion and self-acceptance we all need to grow.

So, what's the secret to all this? Of course, there is no *one* secret, but like most things worth learning, good public speaking and communication happen through a process — learning the fundamentals, discovering the techniques, establishing a training regimen, and practising in front of your peers. Ideally, you should work with coaches and mentors, and along the way accept feedback and guidance — including your own. Through vocal exercises, physical warm-ups, text work and other acting techniques, journaling, meditation, story and editing exercises, real-world practice, and self-assessment — all of which I'm able to teach people in around three to five hour-long sessions — my clients are able to TRANSFORM. But only when they fully appreciate the truth:

Ideas are not enough.
It's how you present your ideas that matters.

Anyone can have an idea, but are you the kind of person who can get other people excited about it, and convince them that you have what it takes to pull it off?

If your answer is:

"Nope."

"Mayyyybe..?" or,

"Yeah, I *think* so..."

then PLEASE KEEP READING — THIS BOOK IS FOR YOU!

In addition to teaching you how to transform your speaking skills to gain confidence, captivate audiences, and grow your career, in the chapters that follow I'll tell my own story of how I went from being an insecure, lonely, depressed and anxious actor who was barely holding on, to being the CEO of a multimillion-dollar coaching company who is recognized by other business leaders and major brands as an expert in my field. Most importantly, after making my own transformation I was able to say, for the first time in my life, "I feel happy and life is good." Honestly, I never thought I'd be able to say that.

All this was made possible through the power of communication — first with myself, and then with others. I'll share some of what I've been through in the hope that you might relate and feel hopeful for *your* future. There are so many damaging and negative things we tell ourselves that keep us from being happy, healthy and successful, but once you begin the process of letting those go, amazing things can happen.

To make you a better speaker than you ever thought possible, I'll share with you the five "Acts" of the OutLoud Method that I teach all my clients, from young entrepreneurs to C-suite executives of Fortune 500 companies. These are:

- **Awareness** — this will open your eyes to your habits and show you how you can control the way you come across in important moments.

- **Articulation** — this will teach you how to tell a good story.
- **Action** — this will help you begin the process of practising, measuring and improving your skills in real-life situations.
- **Alignment** — this will allow you to uncover what is *really* stopping you from becoming who you want to be, emotionally and/or culturally.
- **Automation** — this will teach you the power of practice and give you the essential tools to practice with.

In the final chapter, you will find all you need to make your own Weekly Training Program — think of it as a workout routine for your speaking skills — so you can keep improving for the rest of your life.

You might very well ask: who am I to be telling you all of this? Fair enough. My response would be: if there's one thing I know and am obsessed with, it's helping people get better at public speaking.

I've worked all over the world teaching people to become better communicators. After a sixteen-year career as an actor, starring in films and TV shows from the age of seven and later graduating from the National Theatre School, Canada's premier acting program, I quit the business. I started teaching English, working in Spain, and then became an entrepreneur, founding an education and coaching company in China. All of this led me to co-found my current venture, OutLoud Speakers School, which helps business professionals tell powerful stories and grow their careers and businesses.

Through OutLoud, I've seen people from all different walks of life and levels of confidence and education — some of whom have been through painful, traumatic experiences — transform themselves into *powerful performers* full of passion, precision, poise, and pretty much any other positive p-word you can think of. I've been invited to speak at some of the largest companies in the world, including

Google, Wayfair, Ericsson and ICBC. I've personally coached the founders of multimillion-dollar tech companies, and helped over 3,000 professionals land their dream job, grow their business, and raise over USD$200 million in investment money. I've grown my company's revenue from zero to $300,000 per year, and even been called "Canada's best pitch coach" by the Waterloo Founder Institute, one of the top pre-seed accelerator programs in the world.

All of this is to say, simply — I can help you. You don't have to feel helpless any more when speaking in front of large groups of highly educated people. You don't have to rush through your prepared speech, dying to be done so you can get off stage or turn your video camera off. You don't have to watch peers and colleagues surpass you on the basis of charisma and confidence alone, wishing you could get that promotion, client, or investment you need to take your career to the next level. There is a better way to approach public speaking, and I'm here to show it to you. When you've started working on these skills, you'll be amazed by how much more confident you feel, how much praise you get for your presentations, and how many more opportunities come your way. It all comes from transforming your speaking skills, and that journey begins now.

AWARENESS

To start with, I want you to think about your favourite hobby for a moment.

This should be something you spend hours doing every week or month and love learning more and more about, so you that can get better at it and thus enjoy it more. It could be the guitar (that's one of mine), or cooking (another one for me!), or woodworking (not so much), or knitting, photography, yoga — even *Call of Duty* or *Minecraft* (no judgment!).

Do you remember when you first started learning about this hobby, and began to realize what it takes to become good at it? Do you remember how ignorant you used to be compared to how much you've learned by now, even as you still appreciate how much further you have to go before you're satisfied that you've mastered it? Isn't it wild *how much we don't know*, especially with something new?

This process of *demystifying*, of peeling back the layers of ignorance and brightening your headlamp in the fog of uncertainty, is what Act 1 — Awareness — is all about. You will start to appreciate just how much goes unnoticed by you every day as you communicate with other people.

Self-awareness is often cited as the number-one quality successful leaders need, which was attested to by the results of a survey of seventy-five members of the Stanford Graduate School of Business advisory council.[1] It allows you to play to your strengths, improve on your weaknesses, and see yourself as others see you.

Awareness of others is also critical for success in business (and life as well!). "Why do people do what they do?" is a question we often need to ask ourselves as we navigate the world at large — and for our purposes, we should ask more specifically: "How is the way other people are communicating affecting me, and how can I use that information to adjust the way I communicate with my audience?"

In this chapter, I'll show you how to improve your Awareness about what makes a great speaker, what kind of communicator you are, and how to get *better* at it.

We're going to learn about:

- How to become more AWARE of your physical, vocal, linguistic, and emotional habits
- How to use *mindfulness* (being present) to create the self-awareness you need to assess your public speaking ability
- How to employ the OutLoud Speech Settings, our proven framework for helping business clients with little to no artistic or athletic background learn to control their face, hands, body and voice
- How to WARM UP your body, voice, and mind for a pitch, presentation, or meeting

But before we get into the details of Awareness, I want to share a little of my life story with you, because I hope it will help convince you *why* you need the techniques I'm going to teach you.

---

1 Toegel, G. & Barsoux, J.-L. (2012, March 20). "How to be a better leader." *MIT Sloan Management Review*. https://sloanreview.mit.edu/article/how-to-become-a-better-leader/

My career began way before most people start working. At the ripe old age of seven, I auditioned for an American feature film called *Homecoming*, starring Anne Bancroft, and I happened to book it. I had gotten the opportunity through my father and older sister, who were both in the business, and I inherited their agent, an incredible woman who was well-respected in the industry.

This launched an acting career that lasted through my childhood, with a brief pause during high school so I could be a "normal teenager," as my mum put it. I starred in TV shows and played smaller roles in many feature films. When the time came for me to choose a career, I didn't have to think: I'd already chosen it, and had about a decade head start on all my friends.

I auditioned for the National Theatre School of Canada, and got in (my sister had attended previously, and my father taught there — so I definitely had an extra boost of confidence going in, if not a faith in nepotism). Excited, I prepared to hone my craft and make some industry connections to start my adult life as a professional actor, and, of course, to one day win Oscars, Emmys, Tonys and Golden Globes, and live in L.A. next to Leo and Brad — as you do.

But something was wrong. Well, a couple of things were wrong: namely, my mental health, and the environment of the school. My brother had died in a canoe-tripping accident two years before I started at the school, and I was still experiencing a lot of shock and grief. Compounding my personal problems was a wrongful arrest for aggravated assault: it had taken months of my final year in high school to clear my name and ensure that I didn't go to jail. The trauma of losing my brother, followed three months later by an unexpected and unwarranted criminal charge — and all this at the age of seventeen — made me angry, scared, and self-pitying.

Being at the National Theatre School did nothing to improve my mental health — if anything, the militant and emotionally manipulative teaching methods some of the teachers used made it much worse. They told us that we were lucky to be there, that we didn't know anything, and that we were to accept all their directions without question. They would force us to dance or do movement classes through injury, and make us relive our personal traumas in acting exercises. I witnessed eating disorders, nervous breakdowns, and a threat of suicide while I was there. Although I graduated, the toxic environment I had experienced led me to quit acting altogether, sick of the whole business.

However, upon reflection I'm glad I stuck it out until graduation, because I did learn a lot about my craft. Let me now share some of what I picked up (without the toxicity) — lessons that are essential to improving your awareness of your speaking skills.

BODY AWARENESS

Do you know how an actor prepares or rehearses? How they improve in their craft, and go from the first read of a script to winning an Oscar for their performance? I certainly didn't, until I started studying acting and realized there is so much more to it than learning lines, saying them like they're your own words, and crying on command.

Your whole body, including your face, voice, and even brain, needs to be fantastically well-trained to represent a character on stage or on camera — represent them not just realistically, but *mesmerizingly*, capturing the audience's attention as you work through the moments along your character's journey. It's this kind of captivating and mesmerizing performance that I want you to hold up as your goal when you start speaking in public. You don't have to be Leonardo Di Caprio or Viola Davis, but you'll be surprised how much better than average you can become!

If you're an actor, directors will help you unearth your character's motivations, but they leave the *embodiment* of this character up to you. What that means is, *how the character walks, talks, eats, drinks, smokes, f**ks, yells, cries, laughs and screams* is your choice.

It's the actor's job to understand or invent where your character grew up, what kind of family, class, culture, and environment they come from, and how all that is likely to show up in their face, hands, body and voice. Then, you can start to adjust how you use *your own* body and voice to better represent that character, as well as make the emotions your character experiences — moments of fear, happiness, stress, love, lust, indecision, anger — *clearer* to the audience, and thus more enjoyable to watch.

All acting training, whether it's theatre school, acting classes, studying the greats, or simply working in lots of films and plays, gives an actor an incredible *awareness of their own body.* A skilled and experienced actor can say to themselves while rehearsing, or even in performance: "My eyebrows are furrowed, I should allow them to relax so I don't appear so concerned," or, "I'm sitting kind of slouched over, my character is a military man so he needs a strong back and good posture," or even, "I need to speak louder to get their attention!"

At my company OutLoud Speakers School, where we train entrepreneurs and executives to be powerful communicators, *this* is what we mean by Awareness. It is essential for you or anyone wishing to communicate effectively in public to develop a keen awareness of the way you use your body and voice so you can be better understood, keep an audience's *attention* (arguably today's most valuable resource), and ideally get some of them to do what you want: buy your product, invest in your start-up, donate to your campaign, or follow your recommendation.

To start transforming your speaking skills, and be able to move audiences, you need to start by thinking about what your:

- *voice*,
- *hands*,
- *body*, and
- *face*

are doing moment to moment, and how that might be affecting your audience. Even if your audience is one person, as in a one-to-one meeting or conversation, you should start to do this, as well as noticing *their* habits (although don't forget to listen to what they're saying, too!).

So, how do you start to develop that all-over Awareness? Just by me telling you to do so, right now? Obviously, it's not quite that simple. At school, we spent months on self-awareness, and actors and mystics have practiced the art for years, finding ways to get better and better at it.

But here's where you need to begin: Awareness of your body starts in your mind, because Awareness is just another word for *being mindful*.

MINDFULNESS

While reading this sentence, wherever you're seated, take a second to see if you can notice your breath. As you read this, inhale deeply, and exhale fully. Close your eyes for a moment (I'll be here when you get back) and breathe in and out, fully, three times, paying attention to *nothing but your breath.* Please try it now.

One, two, three...

What you have just done is an example of a *mindfulness* exercise, which is one of the simplest and most powerful practices ever invented by human beings. While most of us likely think of mindfulness as some sort of Eastern practice, like yoga or meditation, that has been watered down and repackaged for the West (especially for the corporate world), as researcher Marion Trousselard tells us, "Contrary to the belief that mindfulness only has Buddhist and Hindu origins, it is also rooted in Jewish, Islamic and Christian religions."[2]

Spiritual disciplines and religions from all over the world place a huge amount of importance on *being quiet, still and paying close attention to what you are doing.* Prayer, meditation, and even dance are examples of this. As I said in the last section, if you want to be an effective public speaker, you need to be aware of yourself and what you are doing, and mindfulness practices are the single most effective (and easiest!) way to start doing that.

Then there are the other benefits of mindfulness, all of which support your mental health and wellbeing, which in turn support your self-confidence, which helps you to improve your speaking skills. Even though I'm not particularly religious or spiritual, I know that scientific data proves that practising mindfulness has numerous and important benefits, including:

---

2 Trousselard, M., Steiler, D., Claverie, D. & Canini, F. (2014, September). "L'histoire de la mindfulness à l'épreuve des données actuelles de la littérature: questions en suspens" [The history of mindfulness put to the test of current scientific data: Unresolved questions]. *L'Encéphale. 40*(6), 474-80. doi: 10.1016/j.encep.2014.08.006

- decreased stress
- illness prevention
- illness recovery
- reduced depressive symptoms
- better focus
- enhanced job satisfaction
- improved academic and work performance
- improved learning and memory
- better mood, self-esteem, empathy, confidence, emotion regulation and ability to pay attention

And that list could go on and on. Mindfulness is like magic, really.

Now, if you're not already sold on mindfulness meditation, this might sound a bit too good to be true. If a friend of yours on Facebook told you there was a vitamin that did all of this, you'd think, "Oh no, Sharon's in a pyramid scheme." But the fact is, there really *is* a practice that takes just 10 minutes a day or less, that requires no money, that can do all these amazing things for your brain and body, and that actually works. Not only that, but it also happens to be *incredible* for public speaking and communication.

In this section I'm going to tell you how you can use mindfulness to increase your *awareness of self and others*, which will lead to better presentations, pitches, meetings, negotiations, conversations, dates (really!), and even the ability to better persuade your kids to eat their goddamn vegetables, already.

A mindfulness meditation you can use

One of the biggest barriers to developing a practice is the number of steps it takes to actually start the thing. For instance, if I want to do yoga, I first have to go to the garage and get out my mat, then clean it, then make a space on the living room floor, then search for a good video on YouTube... and I'm rarely, if ever, going to do all *that*. But if my mat is clean, easily accessible, and there is a space on the floor, I have fewer excuses not to use it.

Likewise, it can be very hard to do an activity without a "follow along" video or audio track, especially if you're just starting out and don't have enough experience with the discipline to create your own practice. I've noticed this with almost every physical practice I've taken up: if I can follow along with someone I trust, I'll do it; if not, I won't.

With all that in mind, I want to make things easy for you. So here is a meditation for you to use to start to develop *awareness* of your breath, voice, mind and body — one of the best possible things you can do as a speaker.

I suggest reading the following passage (an excerpt of the meditation I'm suggesting) through once, to get an idea of what we're going for here. Then, go to the YouTube video that has the audio version of the meditation, which is read by me (in my soothing, only *slightly* nasal baritone) and accompanied by calming music.

Welcome to this mindfulness meditation practice.

My name's Will, and I'll be your meditation guide for the duration of this short practice. Wherever you are, whether you're seated, or lying down, close your eyes and start to notice your breath.

Does it feel tight or shallow? Is it more in your chest or in your abdomen? Try just to notice without changing anything.

Where do you feel your breath?

Is it the cool air in your nostrils as you breathe in through your nose?

Is it the sense of air going into your open mouth?
Or is it in the rising and falling of your belly button?
Again, for now, just notice.
Now you can start to deepen your breath...

This meditation, in its entirety, only takes 5 minutes, and all you need to start is to select the YouTube video by searching:

"TRANSFORM Your Speaking Skills - Mindfulness Meditation"

and sit in a chair and follow along. That's it.

IF YOU CAN FIND TIME TO DO THIS BEFORE your next meeting, presentation or Zoom call, I *guarantee* you will feel:

- calmer,
- less irritable,
- more focused,
- more aware of your breath, body, hands, face, even choice of words, and
- less anxious when speaking in public.

Don't believe me? Then prove me wrong! Try it, and if it doesn't work, please send me a hateful comment on Instagram or LinkedIn, @willgreenblatt. (Or, if it does work, please send me a nice message instead!)

SPEECH AWARENESS

With mindfulness meditation, we've answered the question of *how* to pay attention to ourselves and learned about all the benefits that this provides, like increased focus and happiness. But mindfulness is also a *way of being*, not just a practice. Any time you pay close attention to the present moment, you are being mindful. You can walk, chop vegetables, even brush your teeth mindfully, instead of doing them while thinking about everything you have to do later or what you *should* have said to that asshole in traffic earlier.

By practising *paying attention to what you are doing*, you'll be putting yourself on the road to becoming an immeasurably better public speaker. And this can be done wherever you are, and whatever you're doing. Think less, notice more.

So now that we know *how* to pay attention, the question for someone learning to be a better speaker becomes *what* to pay attention to and *why*. This question runs deep, right to the heart of what makes us human: *What is it about a person that makes us want to listen to them, and trust them?*

Lots of writers have asked this question, with probably the most notable being the prolific and fascinating Malcolm Gladwell. In books like *Outliers: The Story of Success*, he demonstrates that we have a bias toward tall and good-looking people (as well as a host of racial, gender and age biases). In *Talking to Strangers: What We Should Know About the People We Don't Know*, he writes about how people are constantly overestimating their ability to tell who the liars are. My area of interest, however, is looking at the "instrument" of the human body, including the face and voice. Everyone has this instrument, but few of us ever really learn how to "play" it.

Most people have very little awareness of what makes a person

— either themselves or others — effective or not as a communicator. When I hear businesspeople try to analyse a public speaker in my workshops (before I teach them what I'm about to teach you), I'm always slightly amused by the vagueness with which they describe what they saw. I can't count how many times I've heard things like:

"Her tone was kinda off..."
"He was, like, flat, and not really, you know, using the right words..."
"I didn't really understand what they were talking about..."
"It lacked *oomph*!"

The reason that these comments are so vague is that my workshop participants simply don't have the language to describe what they're seeing and hearing. For some reason, the art of public speaking and communication isn't one of the basics we're taught in school, despite how vitally important it is to success in so many areas. So, before you start on your journey to transform *your* speaking skills, you need to know how to describe the way a person is speaking — you need to know what "settings" to look for.

In this section, I'll give you a specific set of things to watch for when you or someone else is speaking: the OutLoud Speech Settings. I'll teach you how to become more aware of these while you're presenting, and how to notice them in others to sharpen your senses and become an expert who is able to help those around you improve their presentations.

When I began coaching, I had very little original content that I would give to my students. Mostly they would practise their presentations with me, and I'd give them tips about what words or gestures to use, or how to loosen up if they seemed tight, but nothing that I could call my own. Then, after being invited to speak to the

Entrepreneurs Organization in New Orleans (a huge breakthrough for my company, which I was insanely underprepared for), I found myself up on stage in front of forty-four CEOs of multimillion-dollar businesses. There I was, in a T-shirt and jeans, with no handouts, no PowerPoint... nothing.

At one point, after working with a volunteer, I told them that they should raise their pitch and volume by a couple of points and slow down their pace. One person raised their hand and said, "Could you write this out for us?" So I turned to a stand with those big sheets of paper, grabbed a permanent marker, and began a sketch of what would turn out to be the following image — an image that we've since used to help over 3,000 individuals and many Fortune 500 companies revolutionize the way they speak to clients, shareholders, and each other. This image represents the 7 Basic Speech Settings, which are fundamental to the OutLoud teaching method.

What Are Your "Speech Settings"?

What does the above image remind you of? When I ask this question in workshops, someone inevitably ventures "mixing board" or "equalizer." And that is exactly right: the Speech Settings are laid out like a sound mixing board, to show how you can *slide* the levels of things like your Volume, Pitch, and Physical Expression up and down as you talk. Just like an audio engineer or a DJ will adjust certain elements of a recording to change the overall *feel* of the song, *you can do the same with your speaking*!

Things like Volume, Pitch, Pace and Physical Expression are all *communicating* things to your audience, whether you mean to or not. Becoming AWARE of where each of your Speech Settings is, moment to moment, and how that may come across to your audience, is the first step in learning to CONTROL your Settings. In turn, this will allow you to use them to *impact* your audience, emphasize different parts of your presentation, and strike the right *emotional tone* for every word.

The 7 Basic Speech Settings

Let's break this down by looking at each of the 7 Basic Speech Settings in detail.

The first five are VOCAL settings:

- **Volume** is how loud or soft you are speaking. For example, to be at a 10 for Volume would be *SHOUTING AS LOUDLY AS YOU CAN*!! And a 1 for Volume would be whispering softly, like the YouTubers in those creepy ASMR videos my wife watches.

  So ask yourself: on a scale of 1 to 10, where do you typically fall for Volume? Has anyone ever told you that you have a "strong" voice, or do people often have trouble hearing you? Also, think about what *adjectives* you generally associate with High Volume (e.g., "confident," "powerful," "angry," "enthusiastic"). What about Low Volume (e.g., "shy," "calm," "laid-back")? Note that you may associate "positive" or "negative" adjectives with each side of the spectrum!

- **Pace** is how fast or slow you're speaking. Some people, like me, speak very quickly: my workshop participants often score me at a 7 or an 8 for Pace. High Pace is especially prevalent in native speakers of "fast-spoken" languages (e.g., Spanish, Hindi, Arabic), as well as people with high energy, those who may be nervous, or some who have just had too much caffeine that day. Other people speak so painfully slowly — at a Pace of 2 or 3 — that you desperately want them to *hurry it up already* and get to the point.

  However, it's important to reiterate that neither side of this coin is "good" or "bad." For now, the point is to just be *aware* of where you tend to fall on these Settings, so that you can learn to make adjustments that will suit particular moments in your talk.

  For example, if you have a lot of corporate sponsors to thank by name at the beginning of a speech, you may want to get through this necessary but potentially boring section rather quickly, so you don't lose your audience. In this case, a nice, respectful Pace of 6 or 7 (which is brisk, but not so fast that you offend the sponsors) will help you get to the interesting parts sooner. And then, when you come to an important sentence in your speech, you can slow down to a 3 or 4 to make sure everyone hears every single, crucial word. (This is also called *emphasis*, which we'll talk about a lot throughout this book.)

- The next setting is **PITCH**, which I'll explain by asking you to think about it in musical terms: the highest "note" you can make with your speaking voice is a 10, the lowest is a 1. Say your own name out loud, right now — where do you think your Pitch is?

Now that you've found your Pitch, let me ask you this: what do you think that a higher or lower Pitch tends to communicate to an audience? Well, like a faster or slower Pace, there are potentially good and bad aspects to both. A High Pitch can communicate excitement, curiosity, and joy, but it could also potentially be read by an audience as an indication that the speaker is childish, or not to be taken seriously. On the other end of the spectrum, a Low Pitch can be interpreted as signalling the authority and confidence of the speaker — but a too-Low Pitch can be boring to listen to!

An important note here: a person's particular Pitch Setting is often associated with male and female stereotypes. Many of our female clients, for good reason, feel that they have been judged because of their High Pitch settings, but have then unfortunately overcorrected by trying to adopt the low, flat tones that their boring male bosses speak in. In general, the point of teaching these Speech Settings is to give people LOTS OF CHOICES, rather than telling them that they need to stick to a certain pattern or completely change "the way I speak" to fit in.

· The **Clarity** Setting measures how much you enunciate your words. Again, there are potential pitfalls at both ends of that 1-to-10 scale: someone who mumbles so much that they're barely intelligible would be a 1, but someone who speaks at a 9 or 10 might sound as though he or she thinks their audience is too stupid to understand what they're saying! However, in my experience, almost *everyone* is too low in Clarity. So one of the best things you can start doing to improve your Speech Settings — *right now!* — is to practise raising your Clarity to an 8 or 9, even if it feels exaggerated

— and especially on the key words of your pitch or presentation (this is also a huge part of *emphasis*). When you
REHEARSE your words with an 8 or 9 for Clarity, chances
are you'll fall on a nice 6 or 7 when you actually deliver your
presentation!

· Next up is **INFLECTION**, which measures the "up-and-down"
movement of your voice — that is, how much RANGE and
MOVEMENT your vocal Pitch goes through in any given sentence (or even word). The difference between an engaging
speaker and a boring speaker often comes down to how
much Inflection they put into their words. An obnoxious radio
DJ might be a 10 ("Heyyyy everyBODY!"), while a monotonous robot (mechanical or human) would be at a 1.

Inflection tends to be the Setting that is least understood.
To help clarify it, think about music again: if your speech was
a song, how interesting or repetitive would it be? Would it
be the same three notes again and again, or would it go up
and down with lots of VARIATION? Variation is key to good
Speech Settings: no matter how LOUD you are, if you stay
at an 8 for Volume the whole time you're talking, people will
get bored of listening to you. According to a paper by Duke
University researchers, "human emotions track changes in
the acoustic environment."[3] So, when it comes to the Vocal
Speech Settings, mix it up!

The five Settings we've covered above are the *Vocal Settings* — what
people generally think of as your "tone of voice." Now, let's look at
the final two of the 7 Basic Speech Settings: your *Physical Settings*.

---

3   https://www.pnas.org/doi/10.1073/pnas.1515087112

Let me tell you: **Physical Expression** — also known as body language — is *so* important, whether you're on a stage, in a Zoom call or virtual webinar, or even in a one-on-one conversation. Can we see your hands gesturing? Is your body *engaged* in your chair or from your standing position? Do you tend to lean forward, toward your audience, or away from them, and how much? Are you using your hands to EMPHASIZE and ILLUSTRATE your key words and ideas?

Some people may be over-expressive with their arms and movement on stage, but in my experience most people are *way* too low on this Setting — so the next time you're presenting, consider sliding your Physical Expression up to a 7 or 8. A good rule of thumb when applying these Speech Settings is: *What feels "over the top" to you will probably look great to an audience, especially if you tend to be low on that Setting!*

Finally, **Facial Expression** is also hugely important, especially when you're in a virtual meeting. The engagement of your eyebrow muscles signifies to the audience that *you* are interested in what you're saying, making it more likely that *they* will be interested in it. So, try notching your Facial Expression up to a 7 or 8 by raising your eyebrows, or furrowing them when talking about something serious, and SMILING when you can!

So there you have it — the 7 Basic OutLoud Speech Settings. These have transformed so many speakers, and I can't wait for you to start playing around with them so that you can feel the results!

Story time:

One of my early clients was a fantastic M.Sc. student at the University of Toronto named Amer, who needed help presenting a research grant proposal worth over $2 million. As a speaker and person he *was full of life, had a big infectious smile, and used his hands and eyebrows to great effect. The whole class couldn't help but smile as he presented. However, all of us had trouble understanding him.*

I told him that his energy was great, and his Physical and Facial Expression were both about 7 or 8, which was awesome. Then I let him know that some of his key words were being lost on us, the audience. At that point, something occurred to me. I asked him how fast he speaks in his mother tongue. He laughed and said, "Very quickly."

As a native Arabic speaker, Amer was used to speaking at a "syllabic rate" much quicker than English (languages like Spanish and Japanese are also much faster than English in general). Also, his complicated, jargon-filled scientific presentation needed to be much slower to be understood, especially given some slight pronunciation issues. So I told him to put his Clarity at a 10, and his Pace at a 2. He thought this was ludicrous, but gamely gave it a go.

What happened was amazing: he slowed down and really enunciated, and although he only was at about a 6 for Clarity and a 4 for Pace, the difference was instantaneous and dramatic, and the whole class burst into applause for how clear and powerful he sounded. And the best part was, he didn't lose his natural Facial and Physical Expression, or his charm — all he needed was an outside eye, and permission to try something new.

PUTTING THIS INTO PRACTICE

So how can you start to implement the Speech Settings framework above?

Here's a homework assignment for you, which I give to every client that I have extended sessions with:

1. Download the PDF of the BLANK Speech Settings at https://outloudnow.com/blank-speech-settings-pdf/ and print it out.

2. Guess where each of your Speech Settings are set at normally (e.g., "I think I'm generally a bit quiet, so I'm probably at a 3 or 4 for Volume").

3. Then, mark your guesses down on the PDF, with a horizontal line representing your "slider" for each Setting (as shown on the image of the Speech Settings at the top of the chapter).

4. Record a video of yourself on your phone. If you don't know what to say, just fill in the blanks of:

   - "My name is..." (*your full name*),
   - "I'm the/a..." (*your job title*),
   - "at..." (*your company*),
   - "and we..." (*description of what your company does*).

5. Watch the video you just recorded (I know, it sucks watching yourself!) and check to see if your guesses on where your Speech Settings were *match* what you now observe when you watch yourself speak on camera.

Apart from working directly with me or another OutLoud coach, this exercise is the first step to realizing the essential principle we teach at OutLoud:

"What it feels like is not always what it looks like."

This bears repeating. I've had clients in my group workshops speak in what the class felt like was a 3 for Volume — so, pretty low — while the speaker truly felt like they were *shouting*! Our senses, while we are speaking, are not to be trusted. It is so hard for someone to know how they come across to others until they have studied the OutLoud Method or done extensive acting training. Watching video of yourself and giving yourself a Speech Setting rating is incredibly useful and insightful. Also, watch other speakers and ask yourself: "What would I give them for Volume? Pace? Pitch?" and so on. And then, "How do I *feel* about that person? Do they appear trustworthy? Confident? Competent? Obnoxious? Arrogant?"

Doing this will help hone your ability to judge other speakers with a more professional eye, like we do as coaches, as well as give you more self-awareness and self-control over your own habits. If you take nothing else away from this book, I hope you realize how important developing this Awareness is for becoming a brilliant speaker and leader.

WARM UP TO COOL DOWN

As we continue our journey through Act 1: Awareness and you start examining your own habits, you might be starting to get even *more* self-conscious. Most of us cringe when we watch ourselves on video. Everybody is surprised at how different they sound on a recording compared to the voice they hear in their head. In fact, while becoming more self-aware, you might find that a lot of memories or feelings are coming up for you: things your parents said about how you should speak and behave; moments when you were teased or bullied for the way you talked; or, as an adult, negative feedback you may have gotten from a boss, or cruel comments about your character from a friend or even a lover.

All of this may be unpleasant, but it's a perfectly normal part of this process. By examining our communication habits, we shine a light on some parts of ourselves we might not love. Public speaking is inextricably tied to our personal identity, and everything we have been told or have experienced about the way we talk is embedded in the Speech Settings we use. The most important thing to remember is something I find myself saying at least once a week to clients:

"Be self-aware; not self-conscious."

But how can I be *self-aware* without being *self-conscious*, you may well ask? Isn't all this analysing of my Speech Settings making things *worse* for my confidence? Don't worry — I have a secret weapon that will help you get out of your head and into your body: a *theatrical warm-up*.

To explain, I'm going to revisit my theatre-school experience with you. One of the reasons I'm glad I stayed at theatre school, despite the toxic environment I mentioned earlier, is because I eventually learned to love things that I had initially hated. One of the most annoying things I had to do at school was WARM UP.

Every day from 8:30 a.m. to 9:00 a.m., and then again before every rehearsal or performance, we were required to roll around on the floor, make ridiculous faces and noises, bounce, swing and jump around, and generally behave like cult members tripping on acid and religious ecstasy.

Often, I'd refuse to participate. I'd put on my leather jacket, go outside, and smoke a cigarette (I was *super*-cool back then), or I'd sit off to the side with my arms crossed, hating everything and everyone. "Why do we have to do this?" I'd think. "This isn't *acting*. None of the professional actors I've ever worked with as a kid did any of this shit; this is just artsy, New Age-y nonsense."

What I came to realize, and now try to communicate to my clients, is that the warm-up is not just a warm-up in the traditional sense of increasing blood flow and body temperature to avoid injury. It's also:

- a physical and vocal exercise routine,
- a mindfulness meditation,
- a chance for breath work,
- dynamic stretching,
- mobility training, and
- a way to practise being okay with looking UTTERLY STUPID!

This last point is key. To continue increasing your awareness of your speaking and presenting skills, you need to get comfortable with looking stupid. It took me a long time to let this lesson sink in, but I now see the value in what my obnoxious-looking classmates were doing as I sat on the sidelines, too cool to even try. And I later learned that all the actors I worked with on film sets *were* doing that stuff — but in the privacy of their trailers!

Warming up your body and voice and getting into the right *mindset* can have a major impact on how you feel, and thus how you speak in public. When I do warm-ups in my workshops or webinars, I'll have participants shout out or write in the Zoom chat how they feel after completing the exercises. These adjectives consistently come up:

- "Energized"
- "Awake"
- "Confident"
- "Present"
- "Calm"

- "Happy"
- even "Silly!"

Why *wouldn't* you want to feel like this when going into a pitch, meeting, or presentation? Why *don't* we all spend 5 minutes right before a big talk to make sure our voice is strong, our mouth muscles are activated, our nerves are settled, and our mind is present?

The answer is because, unlike me and my classmates, no one has ever taught you how to do these things quickly, effectively, *and* explained to you the value in doing them. That was my biggest problem at theatre school: no one ever explained *why* we were doing these absurd exercises, and when I'd ask, they told me to shut up and do the work. For this reason, I always take great pains to explain *why* I'm asking my clients, fully grown adults, to make goofy faces and noises in front of dozens of their peers; I know how hard it is to do these things when you're not clear on *why*.

This is a principle that people studying marketing always learn, but educators all too seldom do: tell people what the *benefits* are (*why* they should do something), not just what you want them to do. (More on this in Act 2: Articulation.)

How to warm up

As I said, I used to *hate* warming up; it seemed so pretentious. But now I always teach my students how to warm up, because of its impact on:

- the *confidence* felt by the speaker, and
- the *energy* felt by the audience.

When I'm coaching someone who sounds flat, uninterested, and just plain boring, I'll often have him or her do a quick vocal or physical warm-up and then try it again. The effect on their performance is immediate and noticeable: I've found that the audience often applauds or shouts out acclaim for the speaker on their second run-through, after they've warmed up properly.

Also, warming up provides a way to get in the right headspace before a big talk, in the same way that LeBron James will ready himself before a big game by stretching and listening to music, or Tony Robbins will psych himself up before jumping onstage at his crazy workshops.[4] The physical and vocal exercises that I'm about to show you will allow you to perform at your best, whether in a pitch, presentation, meeting or interview.

So without further preamble, below are the steps and explanations of the warm-up. (You can skip this section if you want and refer to it later when you're ready to try it out, but there's a lot of useful information here, so I recommend reading it now!)

Step 1. The Body Scan

This is basically a quick version of the meditation we did earlier in the chapter. The point here is to relax your nervous system. We carry a lot of unconscious anxiety and stress throughout the day in the form of racing thoughts ("Oh shit, I forgot to email that person back!" "Is my spouse mad at me? How dare they!") and physical tension and movement (jaw clenched, hands or legs fidgeting, shoulders held high up toward the ears). A quick Body Scan allows us to release tension by focusing on our breathing and body for a little bit, in this case only 15 to 20 seconds.

---

4 Watch *I Am Not Your Guru* on Netflix for a fascinating inside look at this. I'm not a total fanatic of Robbins, but he is undeniably an incredibly effective public speaker.

i. Start by standing up, planting both feet firmly on the floor, and finding some stillness (try to avoid shuffling your feet or rocking back and forth).

ii. Take a deep breath and close your eyes.

iii. Keep breathing deeply, and in your mind's eye, "see" your feet like we did in the meditation — that is, pay special attention to them and how they feel (temperature, tension, sensations etc.).

iv. Slowly move your mind's eye up your legs — through your ankles, calves and shins, knees, thighs, and hips — and then up through your torso. Spend a couple of seconds noticing how each body part feels. Breathe deeply all the while.

v. Open your eyes.

Step 2. Arm Stretch

This one is great for opening the *intercostals*, the muscles beneath the rib cage that expand and contract when we breathe. By stretching these out, we expand our breathing capacity, among other benefits.[5] Not only that, it feels amazing!

i. Stretch both hands overhead, keeping some space between your ears and your shoulders to avoid neck tension.

ii. Grab your left wrist with your right hand.

iii. Lean over to the right side, pulling your left wrist as you lean over to the right. You should really feel a stretch in the *left* side of your body. Lean as far as you can, making about a 45° angle with your legs and upper body. Make sure to keep breathing, and keep your core engaged to protect your spine.

---

5 My voice teachers at school believed we keep emotion "locked" in our intercostal muscles. Weird as it sounds, I saw anecdotal evidence of this at NTS. In voice class, we would stretch our arms out and dig our fingers into the intercostal muscles, like a deep tissue massage. Some of my classmates would quietly weep as they did this. Theatre school was a wild place.

iv. Slowly come back up to centre, switch hands, and do the other side.

Step 3. Belly Breathing

This is the single most powerful *physical defence against stage fright*. When we breathe into our bellies, our nervous system almost immediately calms down. In evolutionary terms, if we were under threat, we would be taking shallow breaths and tensing our upper body to keep our organs protected. By using belly breathing, we are sending the message to our mind and body: "Everything is okay. We're safe."

i. Place one hand horizontally on your chest, just below the collar bone. Place the other over your belly button.
ii. Take a deep breath, and notice which hand is moving more.
iii. If it's the bottom hand, good job! If it's the top, try to see if you can increasingly move your bottom hand as you breathe in and out.[6] Whichever is your instinct, we want to train our belly to EXPAND on the *inhale*, and CONTRACT on the *exhale*, which to many feels counterintuitive.

This technique is also called *diaphragmatic breathing*, because the expansion of the abdomen allows for the diaphragm — a trampoline-like sheet of muscle that lies under the lungs — to descend, thus allowing the lungs to fill up with more air. Lungs are built kind of like medieval wineskins, meaning most of the volume is at the

---

6 In through the nose, out through the mouth is my favourite, in case you were wondering. Some voice teachers differ: in a compelling TED Talk, *Is Your Voice Ruining Your Life?*, Roger Love says that breathing out through your mouth dries out your throat and creates scratchiness, and advocates only breathing through your nose when doing breath work. I doubt it matters much, but give both ways a try if you feel so inclined!

bottom. Belly breathing allows us to take in enough breath to speak powerfully. As my OutLoud co-founder Nicky always says: "Breath is the fuel of the voice." The more you have, the better.

• *Do three to five belly breaths before moving on to the next step*

Step 4. "HMMM-MAHHHS"

This is a singing exercise which will really start to get us weird looks if we're doing it in public. It's useful, however, because it warms up our "resonators" — the parts of our body where sound vibrates when we speak or sing. We have three main resonators in our "vocal instrument": facial, pharyngeal, and chest.

This exercise starts to "wake up" each of these three resonant chambers by having you make a high-pitched "HMM" sound, which starts in the facial resonator, and then open up your mouth to make a "MAH" sound, which starts to vibrate in the pharyngeal resonator and then travels down to the chest resonator as the pitch descends.

   i. Place your hands on your face to feel the vibration.
   ii. Sing a high, loud humming note with your lips together: "HMMMMM." Make this at least a 7 or an 8 for both Pitch and Volume from the Speech Settings (LOUD AND HIGH!).
   iii. Release your lips with a "MAHHH" sound, allowing your voice to descend as you release. Put a hand on your chest to feel the vibration there.

Make sure your "MAHHH" sound lasts for at least a few seconds. If you run out of breath quickly, it means you're wasting breath, therefore not making enough vibration, and your voice is not resonant and strong enough.

- *Do three to five HMM-MAHHs*

Step 5. Big Face, Small Face

This one is even crazier, although thank f**k it's silent! The point here is to wake up the facial muscles — like our eyebrows, cheeks and lips — to help with our Facial Expression.

The way I explain it in my workshops is:

"For Big Face, imagine you're at an airport halfway around the world, and you see your best friend from your hometown. What would you do? You'd go:"

[raises eyebrows, widens eyes, opens mouth, smiles and gasps in delight!]

For Small Face, you're three years old and your mum says you can't have another cookie for dessert, so you go:

[closes eyes, scrunches lips forward and crinkles nose, while grunting in childish anger]

  i. Go back and forth between Big Face (widening your face) and Small Face (scrunching everything up), getting faster and faster.
 ii. Once you've done eight to ten of these back-and-forths, HOLD a Big Face at the end for about five seconds, then release your facial muscles.
iii. Massage, brush and even slap your face to wake yourself up further (I love the face slap, especially when I'm feeling tired!).

Step 6. Tongue Twisters

If you're familiar with the comedy classic *Anchorman*, you'll recognize some of these courtesy of Will Ferrell.

We do tongue twisters to strengthen and activate the "articulator" muscles in our mouths — the muscles that help us pronounce our words. Most of these are found in our lips, tongue and jaw.

The first tongue twister really works the lips: *"Unique New York!"*

i. Say this phrase SLOWLY and CLEARLY, really emphasizing the vowels and consonants.

ii. Say it EVEN SLOWER and MORE CLEARLY! Usually, people are WAY too casual with these tongue twisters; it should feel like work!

iii. One more time, the SLOWEST AND CLEAREST YET!

The second tongue twister is more for the tongue: *"Red leather, yellow leather!"*

Repeat the same steps for this one as you did for the first tongue twister, and then add one more: try to say "red leather, yellow leather" three times FAST but CLEAR (try this now, while you're reading it! Not easy, eh?).

The third tongue twister is to open up the jaw: *"How now, brown cow?"*

i. Relax your jaw, putting your hand on your cheeks to make sure your mouth is open but your face muscles aren't tense.

ii. Remember your belly breathing: take a big breath in, and say "HOW NOW BROWN COW!" as loud as you can.

iii. Bigger breath this time, with an even bigger, longer and louder sound!

iv. One BIG final inhale, and then make the loudest "HOW NOW BROWN COW!!!" you can make, with all the breath, resonance, relaxation and power you've built over this warm-up!

THE END!

Try this before your next big Zoom call or in-person meeting, and *definitely* do it if you have an important talk or pitch. You will feel so much more confident, well-prepared and focused, and it may just make the difference between a yes or a no! It may feel, look, and sound goofy, but trust me — it works!

Remember, the goofiness is part of it: if you can be okay making crazy faces and sounds in front of (or in the room next to) other people, whether strangers, co-workers, or family members, you will be much less easy to embarrass when speaking in public. Coming to grips with weird looks and people laughing at you is a great inoculation against stage fright.

That said, sometimes we really can't make all these noises or faces if we're in a shared office space or interview waiting room. In these cases, I recommend going into the nearest bathroom and doing all of the above exercises *silently,* but breathing and moving as much as you can.

Let's review what we've learned in this chapter:

SUMMARY

- The most important things to start to become aware of when you speak are your hands, face, voice, and body.
- Mindfulness is a basis on which to build awareness of yourself, as well as a hugely beneficial practice that improves your overall wellbeing and, therefore, also helps transform your speaking skills.

- The OutLoud Speech Settings give us a language for assessing both ourselves and other speakers.
- We can use OutLoud's 7 Basic Speech Settings to not only become more *aware* of how we come across as speakers, but also to *adjust* our speech to become better communicators.
- Warming up makes you feel energized, calm, happy and awake.
- The OutLoud warm-up can improve your confidence and effectiveness onstage, so dedicate 5 minutes before your next talk and try it out!

In the next chapter, we're going to change direction a bit. Up to this point, I've tried to teach you to be more aware of your speaking and presenting skills in terms of your physical and vocal habits. But if you're going to transform your speaking skills and make public speaking a key part of your career, you need to know how to tell a *story*.

In the next chapter, we move on to Act 2: Articulation, or *what to say and how to say it.* This one is all about storytelling, and in my opinion, it's as fascinating as it is valuable to your speaking skills. Let's dive in!

ACT 2:

ARTICULATION

In the previous chapter, we covered the basics on how to increase your awareness of the way you come across when you're speaking, equipped you with some tools to assess other speakers, and gave you some tips on warming up so that you can feel calm and confident. The next thing is to just get up there and try it out, right?

Not so fast. Before you start speaking, you need to know *what to say*. You need some content. Even if you have a topic that you know you're going to speak about, like a sales pitch or a weekly report, you need to know how to make the material *memorable*. The same idea can be presented a million different ways. So, before you get up on stage or in front of a camera, let's take a pause to consider the power of story. And I'll start by telling you a little more about *my* story.

When I was ten years old, a girl in my grade 5 class gave a book report that I've never forgotten. She held up a well-worn purple paperback and spoke excitedly about a world where magic was real, and how this boy named Harry finds out he's a wizard and goes to a school named Hogwarts. Some of the kids laughed at her enthusiasm, but I was fascinated. I loved reading fantasy, so I went home and told my mum I wanted to find this book. She had never heard of it, but she took me to the bookstore and there it was: *Harry Potter and the Philosopher's Stone*.

I was completely entranced. The characters, the world, and the story leapt off the page at me, and with my eleventh birthday coming up, I quickly became convinced (truly) that, just like Harry, Hagrid was going to show up on my birthday, tell me I was a wizard, and take me to Hogwarts.

Spoiler: that didn't happen, and though I don't think I've ever had a more miserable birthday as I coped with my irrational disappointment, I stayed a rabid Harry Potter fan all through childhood (and to this day, to be honest). Only after going to theatre school and studying dramatic forms, and years later starting a business around storytelling, did I understand why I and so many others have been obsessed with the global phenomenon of the Harry Potter franchise: it was all about the power of story.

In Act 2: Articulation, we're going to look at why storytelling is so powerful for capturing and keeping attention, and why being clear on your *own* story is so important — not just for business success, but also for your mental wellbeing, believe it or not. I'll also show you the best way to write and deliver *any* story, whether you have to do a self-introduction at a panel discussion, a basic elevator pitch for your company, a stakeholder or sales presentation, or the TED Talk that winds up defining your career.

WHY TELL STORIES?

Stories are so fundamental to our lives that we rarely stop to consider just how deep-rooted they are. From the minute we're born, if we're so lucky, our parents will sing to us of characters who may or may not have existed: babies on treetops, dads buying mockingbirds, and even unnamed narrators pondering the nature of a little star in the sky. From there, we move on to nursery rhymes, then bedtime stories. As we get older, we start to ravenously consume books, movies, music, and TV shows, all of which are fictional narratives. Even reality TV and social media are telling us carefully curated stories, however real they may seem. And all of this is *on top* of listening to our friends and families tell us tales of their experiences as we sip coffee or cocktails, eat dinner, or, as the ancient hunter-gatherers did, lounge around the fire in the cave after a long day's work.

And there's a damn good evolutionary reason for this: human beings simply cannot (and possibly *would not*) exist without stories.

According to *The Storytelling Animal* by Jonathan Gottschall (one of my must-reads for any entrepreneur), human beings are completely addicted to story due to its importance to our ancestors' survival. This brilliant book opens with a story of its own:

Many millennia ago, two tribes of humans lived near each other on the savannahs of Africa. One tribe goes right to bed after a long day of hunting and gathering; the other stays up and tells stories. Which do you think survived?[7]

The answer is, of course, the Storytelling Tribe, of which we are all descendants. And why did they survive? They were able to share *life-saving information*, such as where food and predators may be, in an entertaining, emotionally charged, and therefore *memorable* way.

All of this led to humans' addiction to fiction, art, and various forms of storytelling like theatre and song, which in turn makes every generation of people that much more receptive to information that follows a *certain narrative structure*. Story, as mentioned above, is everywhere.

---

7 Gottschall, J. (2013). *The Storytelling Animal: How Stories Make Us Human*. Mariner Books.

How can you use storytelling to transform your speaking and presentation skills? The first thing we must understand is how a story is *structured*. Once you learn this basic formula, you'll be able to apply it every time you need to write or rewrite anything to do with your business. You can use it for pitch decks, presentations, reports, and TED Talks, as well as marketing materials like brochures, flyers, social media posts and website copy!

Let's look at how a great story works.

THE STRUCTURE OF STORIES: THE HERO'S JOURNEY

In second year at theatre school, we studied with renowned UK director David Latham. He told us about a book called *The Hero with a Thousand Faces* by Joseph Campbell, and took us through some of its key lessons about story structure.

In this influential book, Campbell describes what he calls the *monomyth*, an archetypal "hero's journey" that exists in religious, mythological, and literary classics from around the world and across time. This concept of the Hero's Journey kept coming up for me as I studied TV writing and, later, marketing for my own businesses.

I discuss this concept with almost every single one of my clients, and I teach a condensed version of it as a *template for telling any business story*. The reason is, any time you as a business professional want someone to take any sort of *action* because of your words (like buying your product, following your recommendation, visiting your website, or investing in your company), science has proven that *engaging audiences through stories* is the best way to do so.

Research shows that ads with *character-driven stories* have a predictable measure of success,[8] and neuroscientist Paul J. Zak has shown that character-driven stories consistently cause the brain to make oxytocin,[9] a hormone that encourages us to engage in "cooperative behaviour" such as donating money, continuing to watch an ad, or following a call-to-action at the end of a video.

As a public speaker who wants something from your audience other than applause, you can benefit tremendously from understanding story structure, and the Hero's Journey is the oldest and most reliable structure we have — you can see it in books ranging from *To Kill a Mockingbird* to the Harry Potter series, in movies from *The Lion King* to *The Matrix*, and even in TV shows like *Rick and Morty*. The Hero's Journey takes the story's main character (and therefore the audience) through a series of main plot points,[10] which goes more or less like this:

Our hero lives an ordinary life. One day, the hero gets called to go on some adventure. Initially refuses but eventually accepts after meeting a mentor who agrees to help. Sets out into a new and scary world. Gets in trouble, makes friends, has fights, and so on. Approaches some big climactic moment. Emerges victorious, though at some cost. Heads home, forever changed by the experience. The end.

If you hadn't heard of the Hero's Journey before now, that simplified description above should be ringing some bells for you. In

---

8 Monarth, H. (2014, March 11). "The irresistible power of storytelling as a strategic business tool." *Harvard Business Review*. https://hbr.org/2014/03/the-irresistible-power-of-storytelling-as-a-strategic-business-tool

9 Zak, P. (2013, December 17). "How stories change the brain." *Greater Good Magazine*. https://greatergood.berkeley.edu/article/item/how_stories_change_the_brain

10 The twelve plot points are usually called, in order: *ordinary world, call to adventure, refusal of the call, meeting the mentor, crossing the threshold, tests & allies & enemies, approach the inmost cave, the ordeal, reward/seizing the sword, the road home, resurrection, return with the elixir.*

the next section, I'll show you how to apply this dramatic narrative to anything you write or say, via a condensed, three-part version of the Hero's Journey that will serve as an outline for any presentation or piece of content.

THE 3 MAIN INGREDIENTS OF STORY

As I mentioned above, the Hero's Journey has stuck around for so many centuries because it is a powerful and familiar story structure. Entertainment companies like Disney have built multibillion-dollar movie franchises on the foundation of this structure, and they use it over and over again. So when a story template like this is so readily available, why should you waste time trying to come up with a new narrative structure *every time you try to write a new speech, presentation or pitch?*

By using a distilled version of the Hero's Journey, focusing on just three of its main plot points — what I call the three main ingredients of story — you can make sure your story speaks to people on a deep and primal level, the way storytellers have been doing for thousands of years. This is the structure I use for my clients, from Fortune 500 companies to Silicon Valley tech start-ups, for whom I've helped raise over $250 million in investments. I say that not to boast, but to make clear that this *works*.

The three main ingredients of story are:

1. Problem
2. Solution
3. Prize

That's it. If you cover these three things when you're telling any "business story" (whether a pitch, presentation, team meeting intro, or TED Talk), you will give it so much more *depth* and *breadth* than a boring, chronological recounting of events or a PowerPoint breakdown. I call it Problem>Solution>Prize, or P>S>P. And, yes, you can use this structure for presenting data or processes too!

Let's break it down.

Problem

Identifying a problem is Business 101.

If there's no problem, why would anyone pay for your product or service? If there's no problem, why are we all meeting when this could have been an email? If I don't have a problem I need to solve, why am I listening to your TED Talk?

As professionals, when speaking to an audience, we need to START WITH THE PROBLEM — that is, the reason we're all here. If you're an entrepreneur, it's usually the reason your business exists. If you're a software developer, it's the bug you were working on and the issues it was causing for your app. If you're a manager, it might be a bottleneck in your team's workflow that needs addressing. Whatever the case, you need to set the scene of:

- what the situation is like right now, and
- what the problem is with this current state of affairs.

For those keeping score with the Hero's Journey, the Problem is an amalgam of the "ordinary world" and "call to adventure" plot points. It's everyday life in the Shire for Frodo, which is then thrown into upheaval by the arrival of powerful enemies searching for the Ring of Power, causing him to flee the home he's never left before. It's Harry Potter's drab and miserable life of being neglected, exploited and abused by his aunt and uncle, until he receives that letter from Hogwarts. It's something that your audience (your team, your customers, potential investors, or even humanity as a whole) is going through that is painful or dangerous or at least *less than ideal*, and which needs someone to come along and fix.

Here's an example from a real company whose founder I worked with. I've changed the names and details to respect their privacy, but the essence of the story is the same.

Mohamed was the founder of Robosafe, a company that used robotics to help diagnose and repair dangerous safety hazards on big construction sites. But when he first did his pitch for me, it went something like this:

"Using top-of-the-line AI and machine learning technology, our cutting-edge solution reduces lead times for industrial repairs and minimizes exposure to blah blah blah..."

Now, Mohamed obviously had to be incredibly smart to have created this technology, and it was clear that this company was doing amazing, important things. But the STORY was buried under tech-y, business-y jargon. So I asked him: "Why does your company NEED to exist? Or to put it another way: what bad stuff is happening right now because this technology isn't available?"

He then told me a harrowing story of an explosion on a construction site, and how it could have been prevented with his product. Suddenly, we had our Problem statement! After we rewrote his pitch, the first section now went like this:

"Every day, foremen and workers at industrial sites all over the world face dangerous situations like electrical fires, broken machinery, and even chemical leaks. When they have to repair these things by hand, it can take them hours to get to the danger zone, puts them

directly in harm's way, and can lead to loss of money and even lives."

BOOM. Suddenly, we have a real, urgent, scary Problem on our hands. Now everyone is paying attention, even people who don't work on construction sites, because the problem is set out in a way that anyone can understand it, and think: "Wow, someone should do something about that!"

Once we have established our Problem in a way that is:

- simple,
- clear,
- human, and
- urgent,

we can move on to our SOLUTION — the second part of the P>S>P story. But just before we get to that:

A quick note on the "main character"

I am often asked by clients or audiences who the main character of their story should be. Should it be me, the speaker? The customer? Whoever I'm talking to?

I like to say that, in most cases, the AUDIENCE should be the main character of your story. The reason for this is that they are much more likely to care about what you're saying if, on some level, they identify as the main character in your story. However, that doesn't mean you have to tell the story in the second person (using "you" when speaking to the audience and describing the Problem). You can talk about yourself in the first person if you think the audience will relate to the problem ("I was having a tough time keeping track of my spending") or include the audience and yourself together in the first-person plural ("we"). You hear a lot of this in post-COVID marketing messages: "We are all navigating this new normal," "We're all in this together," etc.

The point is, whomever you choose to talk *about* in your story, make sure whomever you're talking *to* has some interest in the problem at hand, and would therefore be interested in your solution! Speaking of which, back to our P>S>P structure.

Solution

Every problem requires a solution, and that's where YOU come in.

As the founder of a company, the salesperson of a product, the manager of a team, or the speaker on a stage, *people will really listen to you* if you can:

1. Identify their problems in a way they relate to.
2. Demonstrate that you have a Solution.

This part of the story, the Solution, is like the middle (and main) section of the Hero's Journey, where the hero ventures out into the unknown to try to solve the problem that's been introduced. Your Solution should consider the specific pain points of your Problem, and address them one by one in a way that is both clear and exciting.

Let's continue with the story we began above so we can see this in action.

Now that Mohamed had a solid Problem section for his pitch, we needed to clean up the Solution. Part of the issue was, again, too much jargon, but he was also lacking a narrative with which to tie the whole pitch together. He was basically just listing all the features of his robots, but I couldn't understand any of the technical language in a way that made me care — only other engineers in his field would have been able to appreciate it. There was a disconnect with the people who would make up his likely audience when he went out to pitch his business — namely, potential customers and investors.

So, we simplified the Solution section and connected it to the Problem, until it read as follows:

"Using Robosafe's remote control technology, we can take the human out of harm's way *and get to the danger area in less than half the time, saving dollars, equipment and lives."*

For this part of the story, Mohamed didn't have to explain exactly *how* his technology worked; he could prove that his product does what he said it does and answer any technical questions from audience members later on. At this point, the important thing was to show that he had a Solution to the problem that he had already identified.

Mohamed's pitch was now in much better shape, but we still needed an ending. That's where the Prize comes in.

Prize

In Hero's Journey terms, the Prize is called "the Elixir" — this refers to the magic potion, treasure, beautiful maiden/handsome prince, or even just the crucial shift in perspective that is the ultimate reward for the hero at the end of their journey. For our purposes, you can think of it as the answer to this question:

What good things will happen if people listen to you and do as you suggest?

We need the Prize to be the end of our story — something exciting and grand that will make us jump out of our seats and applaud. I often say that the Prize should include the call-to-action for your presentation ("email me," "join us," "if we do this...," "let's...", etc.) so that it creates a sense of hope, excitement, or determination for the future, which is a huge part of the power of story. If you're the founder of a company, it's the vision statement you have on your website (e.g., "a world with no child poverty") that you want to convince investors to put their dollars toward. If you're a manager, it's what you think will motivate your team (e.g., "If we switch to digital, we'll never have to write another one of these reports by hand again!"). If you're making a presentation to shareholders, it's the less immediately exciting but still hotly desired (on their part) statement about how you're going to improve the organization's bottom line (e.g., "We can improve profitability by 13%").

Here's the Prize that we crafted with Mohamed to show his potential clients the benefits of Robosafe:

"Robosafe allows the foremen of North America to know that their crew can go home to their families every night, and that their sites remain safe from disaster. Join us to protect workers and change the construction industry forever!"

The language of the Prize here is emotional, aspirational, big-picture. It gets at the *heart* of what the main character of the story really wants: the peace of mind of knowing that their workers and equipment are safe. In this pitch, the main character of the P>S>P story is Robosafe's target customer, who will decide whether to purchase this product or not. The multimillion-dollar equipment is important, as are the workers' lives, but it's the *anxiety of the decision-makers* about keeping their people safe that provides the emotional pull. Therefore, the true Prize of Robosafe is the *blissful relief* that the foremen of construction sites will enjoy thanks to the reliable Solution it offers to one of their greatest business-related fears.

Additionally — even though they themselves are not the main character in this story — a potential investor in Robosafe, upon hearing this pitch, could still respond emotionally to the rallying cry of "Join us to protect workers and change the construction industry forever!" — especially if, in their minds, they link up the unquestionable good of "protecting workers" with the likelihood that they could get a huge return on their investment!

PUTTING IT ALL TOGETHER

To sum up Mohamed's P>S>P story for Robosafe:

1. **Problem:** dangerous situations on worksites where something is damaged are currently handled by humans who are too slow to get there, resulting in the loss of millions of dollars' worth of equipment and endangering the lives of workers.
2. **Solution:** a remote-controlled robot to repair the damage, keeping humans and expensive equipment safe.
3. **Prize:** peace of mind for foremen everywhere and a safer industry overall.

When the story is told like this, in a structure we recognize, it becomes a no-brainer to invest, purchase, collaborate, or spread the word. This condensed version of the Hero's Journey can help you structure *any* content, pitch, or presentation to maximize its effect on your audience. Give it a try by doing the homework assignment below, and apply this immediately!

Homework:
- Write your business story in 150 to 200 words, keeping it as concise as possible. Even if you're not an entrepreneur, you

can think of it like an elevator pitch, talking about *what you do*, *for whom* and *why*.

- Structure it in the Problem>Solution>Prize format we just covered. Use a Microsoft Word document, so you can take language directly from it for future use; or, take a piece of paper, divide it into three equal sections, and write the Problem, Solution and Prize in plain, urgent, and emotional language.
- When you've finished, post a video of you saying your P>S>P statement out loud to Instagram or LinkedIn; tag me @will-greenblatt and I will review it and give you free feedback!

Okay, now you're armed with a fail-safe story structure. But what about the content? The topic? What specifically should you mention when you're presenting?

Let's dig a little deeper and look at how you can really engage your audience's emotions. Most audiences are usually concerned with the same fundamental things, because, after all, audiences are human beings. There are basically five major concerns that we all share — what I call the Big 5 Human Concerns.

THE BIG 5 HUMAN CONCERNS: HOW TO ENGAGE YOUR AUDIENCE'S EMOTIONS

What do you really want in your life? Is it a family? Lots of money? Long life? All of the above?

In a world of almost eight billion people it can be difficult to remember that, when you get right down to it, we are, all of us, almost laughably predictable. Human beings tend to be focused on the same core things, and whether we are conscious of it or not, advertisers and salespeople have been manipulating us with this knowledge for decades. This was called out by Vance Packard in his 1957 book *The Hidden Persuaders*, in which he explained how ad men used the pioneering psychiatric research of Freud and Jung to manipulate consumers and identify human needs that marketers subliminally play on to sell products.

Now, as Packard points out, the morality of this is highly questionable, and one of the most common objections I get when I ask clients to make their stories more emotionally appealing to an audience is: "I don't want to play on people's emotions for money." Usually, they're concerned about being manipulative, oversharing, or even being judged.

I get that. Many businesspeople are extremely manipulative in the way they present their products, and consciously using stories of personal tragedy or hardships to make people buy something can feel extremely gross.

However, it all depends on WHY you're doing it, and how. You can be honest and vulnerable with an audience without oversharing or manipulating. Telling the difficult parts of your story or explaining how people are affected by the problems you work to solve — i.e., *who you are* and *why you do what you do* — does not have to be done strictly for purposes of profit. Instead, it can open up people's hearts in a way that makes them share similar experiences, or feel touched and inspired to take action for a cause you believe in. But to do this, we need to know *what* to talk about.

As I said above, I believe there are five main things that almost everybody cares about: the Big 5 Human Concerns. Talking about the five topics below in a simple, clear, and emotional way will make people sit up, listen, and ENGAGE.

The Big 5 are:

1. Time
2. Money
3. Health
4. Relationships
5. Emotional wellbeing

I believe that you should always incorporate at least two or three of these concerns in every pitch, presentation, or story. Your Problems, Solutions and Prizes should all be framed around these concerns, and you need to be EXPLICIT about how exactly your P>S>P is addressing them.

Let's look at them one by one.

Time

Does your Problem include WASTED TIME? Does your solution SAVE TIME for your audience? Does it give them MORE TIME to do the things they love?

TV commercials for all kinds of products, from a new type of software to a microwaveable meal, show parents playing with their kids. The narrator will say something like: "*We take care of ___ so you can get back to doing what you love.*"

Here, the product itself is not what appeals to the listener — rather, it's the TIME they get back to spend with their family. As the marketing cliché goes: "Don't sell me the mattress; sell me the good night's sleep."

Money

This one is obvious, especially if you sell business-to-business (B2B) products or services. People and organizations want to SAVE money and make MORE of it.

When I'm pitching OutLoud's coaching services, for example, I make sure I outline clearly how our programs will help the potential client's bottom line. When I give a proposal for our courses to an organization, I start by pointing out that improving communication will improve profitability. According to the Homes report, $26,041 is the "cumulative cost per worker per year due to productivity losses resulting from communications barriers," while conversely, "companies that have leaders who are highly effective communicators had 47% higher total returns to shareholders (compared to least effective leaders)."[11]

So if, after I work with a sales team, even ONE member of that team makes one extra sale because of their newfound confidence, clarity, and speaking skills, then the course has already paid for itself. If every member of the team does, the course has paid for itself five to ten times over. Every business owner in the world will take that deal (provided, of course, you can produce the results!).

And when I work with an individual, I point out the obvious: that "personal branding leads to greater financial rewards" — which is true pretty much whatever you do for a living[12] — and public speaking and storytelling skills are the foundations on which a personal brand is built (unless you're insanely good-looking, and then it doesn't really matter how you talk).

Think about how you can position *your* product, service, charity,

---

11 Grossman, D. (2011, July 16). "The cost of poor communications." *Provoke Media.* https://www.provokemedia.com/latest/article/the-cost-of-poor-communications

12 Close, A., Guidry Moulard, J. & Monroe, K. (2010, October 8). "Establishing human brands: Determinants of placement success for first faculty positions in marketing." *Journal of the Academy of Marketing Science,* 39, 922-941. https://link.springer.com/article/10.1007%2Fs11747-010-0221-6

or recommendation to drive home the fact that it will REWARD YOUR LISTENER WITH MORE MONEY. Even if it seem obvious, remind them. Add facts, figures, and percentages where possible (though be careful not to overpromise and then underdeliver!).

Health

Next up in the Big 5 Human Concerns is physical health.

Many brilliant tech entrepreneurs I've coached have been in "med-tech," developing life-saving technologies. I've also coached many corporate clients in healthcare who provide analysis for medical companies, drug research, fundraising for hospitals, and so on. I'm always amazed by the disconnect between how much their work actually helps people, and what they talk about when discussing or pitching their work.

For example, one of my clients had started a tech company to provide faster response times to heart attacks in Africa. After hearing her pitch and feeling something was missing, I asked her WHY she started the company. She told me that her father had died because a solution like the one she was providing didn't exist, and she founded the company to make sure other families could be spared the grief of losing a loved one due to a preventable cause.

I can't tell you how many times I see this familiar pattern play out:

1. I hear a flat, dull pitch.
2. I ask, "Why did you start this business?"
3. The answer is a deeply personal reason related to saving *lives, limbs, eyes,* or *brain health.*

If your solution *saves lives* or *eases pain*, then tell us *how*. Try not to shy away from sharing details that may be uncomfortable, or too personal. As I said before, including this content doesn't have to be manipulative: if it's part of WHY you do this work, then consider mentioning it as part of your pitch or presentation, especially if it concerns your family.

Which brings us to:

Relationships

This one cuts deep for most people.

We are all social creatures. We have evolved to depend on our tribe for safety, food, and the chance to reproduce. No matter how much technology we have, or how many people live in the city or town around us, the fact that we are social creatures still affects our psychology in a fundamental way.

When you tell a story about a family member, or your spouse, child, or best friend — particularly one that involves conflict or heartache — you'll notice how everyone leans forward in their chair, eyebrows furrowed, lips pursed, listening intently. We can all relate to the bittersweet feeling of an intimate relationship, even if we're single or lonely (perhaps especially so). With few exceptions, we've all had the experience of caring so much about another person's wellbeing that it almost drives us to madness.

Stories of how your product, service or recommendation will genuinely help people get along better with their loved ones or colleagues will always be interesting, because there is almost nothing more important in this world to most humans. Nothing, that is, except for...

Emotional wellbeing

This is it — the biggest of the Big 5 Human Concerns. The one underneath EVERYTHING else. Time, money, health, and relationships don't mean *anything* if a person doesn't feel good about themselves and their life. Consider some of the key factors involved in emotional wellbeing, which, in fact, are the four Human Concerns we've just discussed:

- **Time** does not feel wasted if you're enjoying yourself. Imagine reading a trashy airport thriller for seven hours on a beach in Cancun while you soak up the sun, eat tacos and drink Coronas. (Or, if that sounds like your personal hell, just replace it with something you *do* love!) For me, seven hours of being highly "unproductive" is time well spent.
- **Money** is not a concern if you're lucky enough to not desire it (like ascetic monks), or if you've somehow found a way out of the insidious comparison trap and feel content with how much of it you have compared to others. Many insanely wealthy people take their own lives because they are unhappy despite, or perhaps even because of, all the riches they possess.
- **Health** (physical health) is correlated to mental wellbeing. In fact, the most damaging aspect of physical injury or illness is the psychological toll it takes. For many people, fixing that psychological aspect can lead to a way out of chronic pain, and any product or service that eases suffering invariably focuses on the EMOTIONAL aspect of how happy the sufferer will feel after using it.
- **Relationships** are all about wellbeing: they can sustain us for a lifetime, or damage us so badly we never recover. Any product or service that improves our relationships is really promising to improve our happiness and sense of security.

The Big 5 Human Concerns are just my theory. Take them or leave them as you will, as I have no data to back up my assertions that these are the things people care about; they come from my experience and observation. However, regardless of which of the Big 5 Human Concerns you mention in your business story, always take time to describe the *emotional impact* that your product, service, charity, research, or recommendation will have. While no scientific literature that I can find definitively states what people universally care about, studies *do* show that audiences *take action* when their *emotions have been engaged*.

But if you can, notice how almost anything you find interesting can be traced back to these five topics. And notice how, when you start to incorporate the Big 5 Human Concerns into your presentations (especially Emotional Wellbeing), how much more people start to listen.

Now, let's move on to the final piece of Act 2: Articulation — KNOWING YOUR AUDIENCE.

THE 4 TYPES OF AUDIENCE MEMBERS

So far in this chapter, we've talked about:

- *what* to talk about (the Big 5 Human Concerns), and
- *how to talk about it* (using the 3 Main Ingredients of Story)

but not *for whom*. By this, I mean: WHO is in your audience, and are you properly including all of them in the way you're telling your story?

In this section, I'll describe what I call the 4 Types of Audience Members (or 4TAM, for a completely unnecessary business acronym), and how to reach each one of them. If you understand the 4TAM, you will be able to tell a story that *everyone* will get excited about, not just those people who think like you.

The four types of audience members are:

1. Visionaries
2. Empaths
3. Theorists
4. Pragmatists

This framework is based on the DiSc model of personality,[13] the Unani BioTypes[14] and Kolb's Learning Style Inventory (LSI),[15] as well as my own observation and conversation and the conventional wisdom of others within the start-up community.

While, like all humans, all these types share the Big 5 Human Concerns, each of them differs from the others in some key ways in terms of what *kind* of information speaks to them the most, and will therefore convince them to buy, invest or collaborate.

Instead of a one-by-one breakdown, let's examine the four types together as characters in a story:

In a spotless, futuristic, glass-and-steel Silicon Valley boardroom, four venture capitalists — Viktor, Erica, Ted, and Padma —are waiting to meet a young entrepreneur who has what sounds like a promising idea for a new tech business.

---

13 "Appendix A: DiSC History." (n.d.). https://www.discprofile.com/CMS/media/doc/ed/research/disc-history.pdf

14 Garcia Platas, R., Everett, R. & McElhaney, B. (hosts). *BioTypical: A Mental Health Podcast*. https://open.spotify.com/show/6CZTEvO5UoUX5RTtrOOvcR

15 Kolb, D. (1984). *Experiential Learning: Experience as the Source of Learning and Development*. Prentice-Hall.

The young founder walks through the door, exchanges hand-shakes and pleasantries with the potential investors, sets up her laptop, and then launches into her elevator pitch:

"This is Alia," she says, as the image of a young woman appears on the screen. "Every week, she must travel to town by bus to get essential medicine for her ailing parents. This process is slow and stressful, and leads to a loss of income at the family shop.

"She is not alone: every year, over 40,000 hours are wasted in bus delays in Alia's home country. This results in around $5 million of lost revenue for business owners like her, and the number of people in her situation is growing by 15% year-over-year.

"My company, Quikscoot, provides a cheap and convenient solution for Alia and her countryfolk. Using a prepaid card available at her local market, she can access a locally made electric scooter to drive what is normally a two-hour bus trip in under 40 minutes, due to the bike's ability to squeeze through traffic and travel on small roads. When she gets home, Alia simply returns the bike to its port, all for less than the cost of the bus ticket she otherwise would have had to buy.

"Join me in making Alia and everyone in her country mobile, and change the landscape of travel forever!"[16]

The investors break out in applause, nodding thoughtfully at each other.

Now, here's the question: which investor wound up investing, and why?

Viktor invested because, as a Visionary, he was excited by the idea and story of "changing the landscape of travel forever."

---

16 Extra points if you noticed that this pitch hits *all* of the Big 5 Human Concerns.

Visionaries need a BIG IDEA before they invest in a project or buy something from a company.

Erica invested because she's an Empath. The tale of Alia getting stuck in traffic while trying to buy medicine for her parents struck a chord with her, and she wants to help women like her overcome a difficult situation. Empaths like Erica need a HUMAN STORY.

Ted invested because, as a Theorist, the figures in the story — "40,000 hours wasted," "$5 million lost," "15% growth" — convinced him that, a) Alia had done the research to back up her claims, and b) the numbers told a compelling story of a potential market for this product. Theorists need the DATA.

Finally, Padma invested as well (you guessed it), because, as a Pragmatist, she appreciated the simplicity of the solution: buy a card, get a bike, save time and money. She extrapolated the logistics of what this company needs to work (cost of goods sold, manufacturing, shipping, HR, etc.) and sees that it's a solid operation. Pragmatists need the HOW-TO before they buy in: "How does/will this actually work?"

You need to consider *all four types* to be sure you have covered everyone in the audience. In fact, many organizations train their employees in a version of this framework, such as DiSc, to improve communications. They understand that all of us are different, and if we only speak to people like ourselves we could miss out on up to three-quarters of the population!

Starting now, make sure every pitch or presentation of yours includes:

- BIG IDEAS for the Visionaries in the audience
- HUMAN STORIES for the Empaths
- DATA for the Theorists

- HOW-TO (practical explanations of how things work or will work) for the Pragmatists

Okay, so now we know the value of *story* in human communication and have learned how to *create* a story for any presentation or speech you need to make in your career, to *anyone*. Let's review:

SUMMARY

- As *The Storytelling Animal* teaches us, human beings are "addicted" to story. It's encoded in our genes, as stories helped us share and remember life-or-death information in our hunter-gatherer days.
- The Hero's Journey, as per Joseph Campbell's concept of the *monomyth*, is the most famous story structure, seen in countless books, films and TV shows, including the Harry Potter series, *The Matrix*, *The Lion King*, *The Lord of the Rings* and *Rick and Morty*.
- The Hero's Journey can form the basis of every speech, video, or presentation you make.
- "Character-driven narrative" leads to more "favourable actions" (buying a product, donating to a charity, clicking a link) than simply laying out information, according to *Harvard Business Review*.
- Business is all about PROBLEMS and SOLUTIONS. If you can boil down any pitch or presentation into a problem that you are solving or believe you can solve, then it makes it much clearer, simpler, and more powerful for your audience.

- Your customer's problems are deeper than you may think. Be crystal clear about how you can help your audience solve their *real* problems. (Remember that old advertising formula: "Sell the good night's sleep, not the mattress.")
- To engage your audience's emotions, and therefore make them more likely to listen and remember, include at least three of the Big 5 Human Concerns in every pitch or presentation you make.
- Make sure you talk to *all* of your audience members by including elements that will appeal to Empaths, Visionaries, Theorists *and* Pragmatists. This means offering a solution that includes BIG IDEAS, HUMAN STORIES, DATA and the HOW-TO of your solution.

If you follow these guidelines, you will create a powerful, memorable, and universal story that will resonate with your audience and make them engage with you, share your story with others, and ultimately buy into your vision.

So what's next? Now it's time to take Action, of course. In the next chapter, Act 3: Action, we'll look at putting these steps into practice and getting better at communicating in real, tangible ways.

ACT 3:

ACTION

As a nine-year-old kid, I sang in the High Park Boys Choir of Toronto with my friends Noah and Jacob (who I'm still close with today). We would mess around, make jokes, and play pranks, but we were good singers and natural musicians. (We would later start a pop-punk band called Maximum 40; we had one song, two rehearsals, and never played a gig.) Noah got the solos, and Jacob and I were fine with that: I was always too nervous to do a solo, but I felt okay as long as I could blend in with the choir. Or so I thought.

One night in the dead of winter, we were singing a concert in St. James Cathedral in front of what felt like 20,000 people, but was probably closer to 300. I was singing on autopilot, and I remember looking up at the stained glass and wondering how they made it and put it so high up. Suddenly, I looked out over the crowd, felt a rush of nausea, and proceeded to *throw up* onstage.

I don't think anyone noticed, because I vomited very little and (forgive me here if I'm oversharing) caught it in my hand and disposed of it discreetly. But that didn't stop the nausea, or the kaleidoscopic, syrupy blindness that came across my vision, or the feelings of shame and panic. I didn't know it at the time, but I'd just had my first episode of stage fright.

Now, you might be one of those rare people who's not fazed a bit by standing in front of hundreds of people and delivering a speech or presentation. If you are, then congrats — no need to keep reading! But my guess is that if you *were* one of those people, you probably wouldn't have picked this book up in the first place. Public speaking is a very common fear,[17] so there's a good chance that, like me and almost every single one of the over 4,500 people I've coached, you experience *some* form of performance anxiety, social phobia, or stage fright. Even if it feels mild, the anxiety that so often accompanies public speaking gets in our way by distracting our thoughts, drying out our vocal chords, causing us to rub sweaty palms on our clothes, restricting our ability to breathe deeply, and making us forget what we wanted to say.

In this section, we are going to tackle everything a speaker needs to do the job of performing, *on stage or on camera,* and *in the moment.* What does it take to override the type of panic I felt as a small boy (and that I still feel on stage or before a big presentation)? Then, how does a speaker perform, assess, rehearse, and improve?

The best way, like anything, is to just *get up there and do it.* All the theory in the world is useless if we don't put it into practice. So now, let's take some Action.

SAY YES TO THE STRESS

For some reason, my stage fright when performing music is much worse than when performing as an actor. Maybe it's the fact that I

---

17 Although it's not the number-one fear, as many communication coaches claim; percentages differ, but many studies, like one done in Sweden, have identified it in around 25% of people surveyed. Furmark, T., Tillfors, M., Everz, P., Marteinsdottir, I., Gefvert, O. & Fredrikson, M. (1999, August). "Social phobia in the general population: Prevalence and sociodemographic profile." *Social Psychiatry and Psychiatric Epidemiology, 34*(8),416-424. 10.1007/s001270050163

care more deeply about music, or that singing is inherently a more vulnerable act than speaking. But I think the truth is that I have way more experience on stage as an actor than as a musician.

As an actor, I've performed almost a thousand nights on stage and many more days on set in front of the camera. I've done workshops and readings and countless auditions, and while the fear never really goes away, I've developed a million-and-one lessons, tips, tricks, and psychological safety nets to keep me from freezing up too badly while performing.

For you, as a professional, there are countless opportunities in the public speaking arena, as well as daily moments for you to speak up and share your ideas: meetings, brainstorming sessions, social media content creation, public talks, pitches, or presentations. Saying yes to every opportunity to work with people who are powerful communicators, and being unafraid to be the "worst" speaker in the room or on the stage, will ultimately make you into one of the best.

So, the first takeaway of this chapter is: say YES to every single speaking opportunity you get. Presentation at work? Yes. Podcast appearance? You bet. Panel on global climate policy? Absolutely, I feel *totally* qualified for that!

Feel the fear, and then do it anyway. Build the plane on the way down. Fake it till you make it. Say yes to the dress. Use whatever cliché you like that describes this attitude of taking opportunities you might not feel ready for, but know they are the fastest way to build confidence as a speaker — not to mention the career opportunities that almost always come from speaking in public, like leads, connections, and more speaking engagements! You can see the virtuous cycle below:

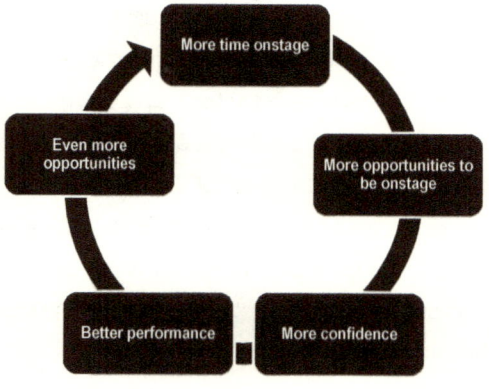

If you don't believe in jumping right in the deep end with your public speaking and presenting, let me tell you about the first speaking gig I did after starting my company OutLoud: an unpaid appearance at a wild and wacky fitness/business event run by the phenomenal entrepreneur and fitness trainer Julian Ho.

I remember feeling disgruntled that I wasn't being paid, but resolving to use the opportunity as a learning experience. After I did my thing (which, if you've attended one of my workshops, you know is an energetic, interactive, and physically demanding experience), a striking businesswoman named Julie pulled me aside.

"I love what you did up there, and I think you'd be great for an event I'm hosting in New Orleans," she said. "Unfortunately, we can only pay you $1,700, plus expenses and accommodation. Is that okay?"

I'd never charged more than $50 per hour for my work at the time. I was inwardly celebrating, but tried to play it cool. "Yeah, that's no problem," I replied, with feigned casualness.

"Are you available February 6th and 7th?" she asked.

I knew I wasn't. "Yep, that sounds good!" I said. I had to get my OutLoud co-founder Nicky to cover for me, but after that, I was on my way to the US for my first paid speaking engagement!

When I got to New Orleans, I felt intensely that I was not supposed to be there. The hotel was fancy, and the attendees of the event were all entrepreneurs whose businesses made over $1 million per year. They were there to work on their speaking skills when training other entrepreneurs, who were part of a business accelerator program that you could only join if you made at least $250K per year. I was convinced that the fact that I was a guest speaker at this event was some kind of a horrible mistake, and I started to panic as my moment approached.

I was wearing jeans and a *Star Wars* T-shirt (*why*?!). I had no PowerPoint presentation, no handouts, no nothing. I stood at the front of the room and began to speak. In one awful moment, my cell phone rang in my pocket. I pulled it out, silenced it, and kept talking as if nothing had happened (which turned out to be the right move).

Even though I was completely underprepared, my weird hybrid of lecturing and live coaching ultimately went over well, and I ended up getting several other speaking engagements thanks to that New Orleans event. Not only that, but my work was also validated by my target market, and as a bonus, many of the older founders there gave me priceless advice on growing my business and improving my talk as we ate and drank together in one of the coolest cities in the US. The organization I spoke at has been one of my most reliable customers and networking hubs to this day. All of this happened because I said yes to an unpaid speaking gig in downtown Toronto, and then went to New Orleans on a wing and a prayer.

LOWER THE STAKES, LOWER YOUR FEAR

By now, you may be thinking: "It's all very well for you to talk about your lucky successes, but the idea of doing that — just getting up there before I've adequately prepared — makes me uncomfortable at best, and at worst freaks me the f**k out!" If so, I hear you.

As I've explained, I know firsthand what stage fright is, and I can empathize. But there are some key lessons I've learned over the years about how to deal with it, the first of which I'll share with you right away.

One of my favourite genres of fiction is heroic fantasy. As you can probably tell from my obsession with the Hero's Journey, I love the stories in books like *Harry Potter* and the *Lord of the Rings* series, with flawed characters battling unimaginable odds and revealing the best and worst of humanity along the way.

My favourite author in this genre (aside from J.K. Rowling) is David Gemmell. Although he's sometimes criticized as being too macho or writing overly terse prose, in my opinion he creates impeccable characters and dialogue. One of my favourite scenes comes from his novel *Waylander*, a tale about a deeply flawed anti-hero whose family was murdered. After his family's death, Waylander becomes an assassin and finds himself protecting a young woman called Danyal and two children amidst a bloody civil war — a war started by an assassination that he carried out.

One night, while the children are sleeping, Danyal asks Waylander to teach her how to be calm like him in situations of extreme stress. She says she'll need to know how to defend the children if he is killed, and she admires how steady he is after they've survived several deadly encounters together; they've also begun to feel romantic interest for each other by this point, which is important context for the next scene (I've paraphrased this sequence below for brevity and clarity),

After reluctantly agreeing to teach Danyal his secret for staying calm in the face of danger, Waylander picks up a pebble and asks her to catch it when he throws it to her. He tosses it and she catches it, no problem. She throws it back and says, "That was easy. Why are you showing me this?"

He explains, "I'm going to throw it again. And if you miss it, I will walk away from you and the children tonight."

She begs him not to do it, but he throws the pebble, and wildly she lunges out, fumbling with it before she finally catches it. She yells at him, "What's the matter with you? Why would you do that? Answer me!"

"Only if you tell me what you did."

"I did what you asked me to do," she replies.

"No, that's not what you did."

"I stopped you from leaving us?"

"That's not it either."

She thinks, and then she responds with a smile, "I caught a pebble in the moonlight."

I absolutely love this scene, and Danyal's final line has stayed with me ever since I read it. To this day, the lesson that I distilled from this scene — "Lower the stakes" — is one of the most useful pieces of advice I give myself and others, and it has remarkable power.

When our brain perceives a situation as "important," our ancient nervous system — so well designed for helping us avoid imminent threats — kicks into fight-or-flight mode. And for many people, the prospect of public speaking can be a trigger for this deeply wired impulse. According to *Psychology Today*, "Many people overestimate the stakes of communicating their ideas in front of others, viewing the speaking event as a potential threat to their credibility, image, and chance to reach an audience."[18]

As we've discussed, fear of public speaking is linked in our instincts to fear of death, ostracization, or loss of status within our tribe. However, simply knowing this may not be enough to help avoid that overreaction from our minds and bodies. So here is a thought exercise you can use to "lower the stakes," and thus help dampen your fear.

When you're feeling nervous about an upcoming public speaking event, ask yourself a series of questions — out loud, if you're not too embarrassed — and then respond to them for yourself. Once you get the hang of this technique these types of questions become easy to think up for yourself, but for now, start with these:

- "Will I lose my job if this talk doesn't go well?"
- "Will I have to give up my business?"
- "Will I lose the respect of my audience forever?"
- "If it *does* go poorly, can I learn something from that?"
- "Have I ever given a talk before that went so badly I couldn't recover from it?"
- "What happened the last time I was nervous for something like this? Did it go better than expected?"
- "Does my audience know what I'm talking about better than I do?"
- "Is everybody in my audience likely to judge my performance as harshly as me?"

18 Tsaousides, T. (2017, November 27). "Why are we scared of public speaking?" *Psychology Today*. https://www.psychologytoday.com/ca/blog/smashing-the-brainblocks/201711/why-are-we-scared-public-speaking

- "Are they normal humans who burp, fart, pee and experience occasional diarrhea, just like me, maybe making them a little less intimidating?"
- "Will I remember this moment in a month? In a year? In five years?"
- "Is *this really a big deal in the overall story of my life*?"

Chances are you instinctively *knew* the answers to these questions were an obvious YES or NO (with maybe some exceptions). But the message of this exercise is to remind yourself of *five truths about stage fright*:

1. Worst-case scenarios rarely come true.
2. Your presentation usually goes better than you think.
3. The audience is filled with mere mortals just like you.
4. Any "failure," if it does happen, is a learning experience.
5. In the long term, your presentation is probably insignificant to your life.

MAKE VIDEOS. OFTEN. NOW.

By now, I hope you can see the value in saying yes to any and all speaking opportunities, and lowering the stakes of them in your mind to fight against stage fright. "But what if I don't get offered any speaking gigs?" you may ask. The fact is, you might not have any connections with event managers, or know how to develop them. So, how can you find speaking opportunities when none seem accessible?

There are lots of people out there promising to teach you how to find and book paid speaking gigs, and in my personal and painful experience, none of them work. There may be those out there who can help you, and if you find them, please let me know (@willgreenblatt). But for now, I recommend another approach.

While speaking on a stage in front of a live audience is a fantastic way to gain experience, learn to manage stage fright and hone your speaking skills, it's not the only way. Lacking connections is no longer a barrier to getting your message out there in the era of online communication.

Let me tell you about what happened back in early 2020, when the world was falling apart. I'd started my company OutLoud three years prior, and was flying around the world doing speaking gigs and coaching, as well as running events, workshops and classes in Toronto. Then the pandemic hit, and we were all on lockdown. I lost about $35,000 worth of contracts in a single week when all our in-person workshops were cancelled, and I started to think my company was finished; this thing I'd come to regard almost as my baby was going to die before it even had a chance to grow.

I spent about a month in a deep depression, as many of us did, until a conversation with my then-mentor Mike Reid, of Dent Global, helped snap me out of it. He said something to the effect of: "You're an entrepreneur. Are you going to let this problem stop you, or are you going to be the one to solve it, and help your clients solve it too?"

The thing I realized — my "pivot" — was this: "Everybody is in lockdown, but people still need to talk to each other. How are they going to do it, and how can I help them with that?" I had already been doing online coaching, so we pivoted our business to VIRTUAL COMMUNICATION COACHING. This turned out to be the right move, but I needed a way to get the word out there and get some new clients.

After having resisted it for the first three years of my business,

I finally started *making videos* and *posting them on social media* to make up for the leads I wasn't getting from in-person events. In the first few videos, each of which took me at least two hours to create and edit, I spoke about:

- dealing with the stress of lockdown,
- how to communicate on Zoom,
- how to use Facial and Physical Expression on video,
- why storytelling was still important,

and many of the other things I cover in this book. Luckily, I didn't have any clients at the time, so I could dedicate time to learning what worked, what tools I could use, what kind of content resonated, and how to be more efficient in creating and posting these videos.

Now, after over two years of learning the hard way, I want to share with you what I learned and give you my recipe for making content, which has grown my followers by over 600%, led to thousands of dollars' worth of sales and countless opportunities, and created immeasurable *credibility* in the eyes of potential customers. I've heard several customers tell me they decided to hire my company only after checking out my stuff on social media.

And that makes sense, doesn't it? We buy from people we know. Either we knew them already, or we've had a few sales conversations with them, or we spend time *watching and listening* to them online, to the point where it *feels* like we know them and are ready to buy.

It's what Mike, my mentor who inspired me to start, calls being "pre-sold": when a customer calls *you* and just *has* to work with you because they've been so impressed by your content. This can happen through publishing a book, giving a TED Talk, or having a great website or brochure, but in my opinion the easiest way to create this kind of consumer trust is through *short, low-maintenance videos.* And the only way to do that is to just get started.

I have a maxim I repeat ad nauseam: "Make videos. Often. Now." What you can do, right now, is just *start*, however inexperienced you are, and build toward a habit of CONSISTENT CONTENT CREATION.

Which begs the question: "How should I do that?" Whether you have never done it before or are already engaged in content creation on some level, chances are that putting yourself on video is a hassle you'd rather avoid due to how much work it seems like. (If you're already a content master, I recommend reading the following sections anyway to learn about how to incorporate these lessons into your current content and workflow. But if this is all old news to you, feel free to skip ahead to the next chapter, Act 4: Alignment.)

Action is always the hardest part of my programs — both for me, in deciding what to teach my clients when they may have different needs for their jobs, and for my clients, when they start to take this theoretical knowledge and apply it in real-life scenarios. However, the thing I find myself constantly coming back to is: "Make videos. Often. Now." The reason is:

Video content creation is like a training ground to hone your public speaking and storytelling skills.

If you challenge yourself to make videos constantly, you are building the habits of talking about yourself and your topic in *clearer* and more *concise* terms; you're training yourself to *structure* information in a way that engages an audience (the engagement analytics of social media will tell you if you've done this); and you are practising remaining *confident* and *articulate* when that little light turns on and it's time for "action." This is a skill set every leader and speaker needs, and committing to making social media video posts weekly, or even daily, will force you to keep progressing, as well as provide you with many great opportunities and keep you top of mind for potential customers, employers, or investors in your network.

If you're like I was, initially reluctant to post on social media, I hope to both convince you that you *can* make consistent content to help yourself and your company *without* losing your dignity and sanity, and show you how to do so. Believe me, I understand that posting videos is scary, but there are ways to overcome that fear. Let's look at a couple of these before we go on to the details of actually making a video.

A GOOD PROBLEM TO HAVE

In today's hyperconnected "cancel culture," it's easy to feel that we're living in a fishbowl where our every move online is scrutinized. When I hit "publish" on my first LinkedIn video, I felt a wave of panic, and the thoughts that came rushing in included:

- "Who is going to see this?"
- "What will they think of me?"
- "What if I said something wrong, stupid or offensive?"
- "Did I just ruin my reputation?"

Then I waited. The video got about fifty views and three likes. The realization hit me:

If enough people are paying attention to you that your words are causing a significant reaction, that's a great problem that very few business owners have.

Nobody cares about your little video. At first, nobody will even watch it — until one day, they do. Then a few more do. Then people start commenting. They message you and compliment you on your content. They start sharing your words, then other people find you, and growth starts happening. People start reaching out to you because they want to hire you or buy your products. Some will say negative things, and that's okay! If you keep doing it, you get better and better as you get bigger and bigger, and you will feel stronger and less intimidated about putting your face, voice, and ideas out there.

In an interview clip on YouTube, Ed Sheeran uses an analogy I love and quote often. Speaking of starting out as a songwriter, he advises: "View [songwriting] as a dirty tap. When you switch the tap on, it's just gonna be shit water coming out, for, like, a substantial amount of time, and then eventually clean water will start flowing. Once in a while, some shit will still come out of you, but as long as you leave the tap running, it's fine."[19]

What you need to realize, as a person trying to make a living in the 21st century, is that you are a *brand*, whether you like it or not and whether you intentionally post online or not. Those who create content get attention and can live the lives they want once they scale their businesses or get promoted. But to get good at creating content, you Just. Have. To. Start. (Or *re*start, if you've lost momentum or inspiration.)

Make videos. Often. Now. Or, to paraphrase Ed Sheeran: "Open the tap and keep it running."

---

19 https://www.youtube.com/watch?v=RDyg_41QF1w&t=59s

HOW TO MAKE VIDEOS

Hopefully, you've now been convinced to start making videos consistently. You believe that making at least one video a week will sharpen your speaking skills and grow your business and/or your personal brand, especially if you post them on social media.

But perhaps you still have some questions, like:

- What do I talk about?
- How long should the videos be?
- Should I write a script?
- How long should it take me?
- What equipment do I need?
- How do I edit the videos?
- Where and when should I post them?

These are all great questions, so I'll go through them one by one.

What do I talk about?

What are the PROBLEMS your audience has? What are some SOLUTIONS you have for those problems? What is the PRIZE they get if they follow your advice?

This is what we covered in Act 2: Articulation, when we looked at how to structure your pitch or presentation: P>S>P. But really, the same formula is applicable for EVERY PIECE OF CONTENT YOU MAKE.

The easiest thing to do is pick a Problem first,
and then turn it into a headline.

For example, let's say you're an entrepreneur whose software helps online stores find customers. Who's your audience? E-commerce business owners and their marketers. Their Problem? Attracting attention and making sales.

There are a million little things that can create difficulties for finding customers for an online store, such as:

- Where to host your store
- How to write great marketing copy
- What kind of pictures help sell your goods faster
- How your landing page should be structured to improve conversion rate
- What font and colours to use for your branding
- How to bundle products to increase sales
- Email marketing vs. content marketing
- How to handle refund requests without angering clients
- That list could go on and on. And if you think about it, every single one of those problems could be the HEADLINE OF A VIDEO POST!

Pick a problem your customers have — for example, "how to write great marketing copy" — and let your customers know it's for *them*. So the *headline* of your post (what you title the video on YouTube, or write in the FIRST LINE OF THE CAPTION on other social platforms) would be:

"How to write great marketing copy for online stores"

That's a totally decent headline, although we can make a couple of changes. "Great" is a generic word; what does this great copy ACHIEVE?

"How to write copy *that converts* for online stores"

Your audience wants their content to convert, not just "be great," so this is a good adjustment. Also, "marketing copy" is probably redundant, so I took out the word "marketing"; we understand what "copy" means in this context.

And one more thing: are your customers' online stores in Canada, or the US? Are they elsewhere? Are they in a specific industry? Do they have to be above or below a certain size or revenue marker?

Once you have that targeted sense of your audience (what social media marketers call your *niche*), you can add language for them:

"How to write copy that converts for online stores in Canada"

BOOM — we have our topic. You can do this every day and never run out of things to talk about, as well as reposting content that does well or creating new videos on old topics that people frequently want help with. Coming up with a great headline is an art on its own, but this should get you started.[20]

Next question:

How long should the videos be?

Sixty seconds. This is the length I always recommend, for many reasons:

- It's short and sweet, but long enough to provide value.
- You don't have to write or memorize too much.

---

20 To get better at writing attention-grabbing headlines, my personal favourite resource is the "Harry's Marketing Examples" newsletter. Google it and sign up for great inspiration on how to make your marketing copy, including headlines, better. I don't know Harry, or make any money off his newsletter — I just love it.

- It's the perfect length for platforms/features like TikTok and Instagram Reels, and a good length for YouTube Shorts and LinkedIn, which at the time of writing are some of the fastest-growing and most viral social video formats.
- You can usually do a video in one take.
- People have short attention spans, and unfortunately, 60 seconds is still pushing it.

Try 60-second videos for now, and you can always go longer or shorter as you become more familiar with the process.

Should I write a script?

That depends: are you a MEMORIZER or an IMPROVISER?

Memorizers are people who need a written script to perform at their best, and feel almost naked without a clear text or set of bullet points to work from.

Then there are the Improvisers, who hate memorizing things and feel much better winging it or making it up on the fly.

Whichever one you feel you are, even if it's a mix of both, try both ways and see what works for you! Write a script and memorize it, then try improvising for your next video, and see which one feels better.

Making videos, like speaking to a live audience, is a process of constant improvement and experimentation. So, stay open and curious!

How long should it take me?

When I started making videos at the beginning of the pandemic I had no clients, because they had all cancelled our in-person sessions, so with all my free time, I used to spend two to three hours per video. But that is a ridiculous amount of time for any entrepreneur or businessperson whose job is not video creation exclusively, and now that I know better I want to help you avoid it. Now, it takes me only 30 minutes to,

- make a video,
- edit it, and
- post it to three different channels (I use Instagram, LinkedIn and TikTok).

If you follow my recommendation of making 60-second videos, pointing the camera at yourself and talking, it may take you longer at first — especially as you iron out the kinks in your performance and editing skills — but eventually it should only take 15 to 30 minutes to create a video. And no matter how crazy life gets, if you truly want to succeed, you'll be able to find the time.[21]

What equipment do I need?

A smartphone and a tripod, if you don't have anywhere to prop up your phone. A window to create natural light (shoot in the daytime and you'll look great). Use a background with some nice books, plants and art if you have it. No microphone necessary.

Once you get going, you can start to invest in things like lav mics and soft box lights, stands and thousand-dollar cameras, but at first, just use your phone! And keep in mind that, according to HubSpot Research, "consumers and customers prefer lower-quality,

---

21 For those of you with kids who may be screaming at me right now, I know plenty of content creators with multiple children who also run large companies and have rich personal lives. Like everything, it's a matter of priorities!

'authentic' video (like those shot on smartphones) over high-quality video that seems artificial and inauthentic."[22]

Shoot in vertical mode so you can post on Reels, TikTok and YT shorts. This 9:16 aspect ratio is perfect for mobile viewers, who are becoming more and more of our online audience — so optimize for mobile!

How do I edit them?

There are many apps that content creators use to make their videos fun and professional-looking. However, with this "point and shoot" format I'm proposing, where you face the camera toward you and speak into it in one take, you can simply trim the beginning and end and add text or subtitles, music and effects, all *inside the apps you're uploading on*. Even LinkedIn, which was late to the party until recently, has added a "trim clips" feature to its video uploading software.

If you like, you can also Google "How do I edit videos on TikTok/Instagram/LinkedIn," etc. That's how I learned everything I know, as well as by just doing it. As Marie Forleo, entrepreneur and creator of MarieTV, tells us in the title of her book: *Everything is Figureoutable*.

To learn more, start doing! The more you do it, the faster you will get.

However, if you do want a more professional look to your videos and you have a bit of a budget, hire an editor! Sites like Upwork and Fiverr have brilliant young editors from all around the world who need to build their portfolios and will happily work for insanely cheap rates. I got my first-ever pieces of content edited for ten bucks a video!

---

22 Collins, A. & Conley, M. (2022, May 24). "The ultimate guide to video marketing." https://blog.hubspot.com/marketing/video-marketing

If you're using a third-party editor, make sure you ask them for:

- music,
- b roll,
- captions,
- graphics, and
- jump cuts.

They should do this anyway, but it's best to be clear about what you want. All of these will add a professional look to your content, and you'll be amazed at how wise and confident you look and sound when an editor gets done with you!

Finally:

Where and when should I post them?

Where you should post your videos entirely depends on *where your paying customers or whoever you want to reach spend their time online.* Is it Facebook? Post there. YouTube? Post there. For now, choose ONE, but make sure it's the right one! Many platforms are segmented by demographics. For instance, in 2021 users under thirty are 63% more likely to use Snapchat than those sixty-five and up; those with bachelor's degrees or higher are five times more likely to use LinkedIn than those with high school diplomas or lower, and 46% of women use Pinterest compared with 16% of men.[23]

This data can help you find who you're looking for, but unless you already have a sense of what social media your potential customers consume, do some more research and then choose *one* channel and go all in!

---

23 Pew Research Center (2021, April 7). "Social media use in 2021." *Pew Research Center.* https://www.pewresearch.org/2021/04/07/social-media-use-in-2021-3/

Social media algorithms reward certain behaviours, especially those that fit into the culture and the parameters they've set out for their users. When you make content for a certain platform, you learn what the app "likes," and therefore what it will boost to many people to help you grow your reach. You'll also learn what the app doesn't like, which will keep you stuck and stagnant. Choosing one channel will allow you to master one set of rules before trying to tackle another.

Once you've been posting for a few weeks, use the "Insights" or "Analytics" on your chosen platform to make sure the people you THINK your content is for are actually engaging with it! Keep open about this: for instance, you might think your content is for men, but then find that women are liking, commenting on, and sharing it more!

How about *when* to post? That also depends on where your customers are, geographically speaking. If they're in Toronto, don't post at 1:00 a.m. EST, when most of your customers will be in bed and not checking their phones. There is data available about when people like to check their apps, so Google this information and experiment until you find a good time of day. Again, once you've started to post, use the Insights/Analytics to find out what time your users are engaging the most, and consciously post at those times!

In terms of frequency, START WITH ONE VIDEO A WEEK (minimum). Pick a time in your schedule to create, edit and post (writing a caption and adding hashtags takes time, too). Once you commit to that, and your content creation gets easier, try three times a week. Once that becomes habitual, try for ONCE A DAY (intimidating though that may be), setting aside 15 to 30 minutes to film, edit, caption and post. Some experts believe three to five posts a day is the goal, but in my opinion, unless you're trying to grow your

Instagram or LinkedIn channel as your main source of marketing, nobody has time for that! Also, bear in mind that many of these "social gurus" are posting images, quotes, and memes as well as videos, so it's easier to be prolific.

One video a week will put you well above your competition in terms of output, traffic, speaking skills and credibility. You'll get more and more confident in your talking points, performance, and storytelling ability, and you'll find that business opportunities are discovering YOU instead of the other way around.

No time like the present. Make videos. Often. Now.

Let's review Act 3: Action:

SUMMARY

- Say yes to speaking gigs, chances to present at work, and speak up more in group meetings. No matter how small, see any unpaid gig as a way to practise without needing to deliver a masterful talk.
- Don't worry about being perfect or totally prepared.
- Start posting on social media. Make videos. Often. Now.
- Lower the stakes for yourself, on video or when speaking live, by reminding yourself of the *five truths about stage fright:*
    > Worst-case scenarios rarely come true.
    > Your presentation usually goes better than you think.
    > The audience is filled with mere mortals, just like you.
    > Any "failure," if it does happen, is a learning experience.
    > In the long term, your presentation is probably insignificant.

- Don't worry about anyone negatively reacting to or commenting on your videos. No one cares, and if they do, that's a good problem to have.
- The first few videos you make will probably be bad, and that's okay! You need to make those ones to get better and start making your good videos. As Ed Sheeran says, "open the tap."
- Make 60-second videos, shot *vertically* for mobile/social media, with a tripod and natural light, no mic necessary, talking about problems that your customers have and how to solve them.
- Choose one channel and post the videos there. If you can, use the in-app editor, but if you have some dollars, hire a cheap editor on Upwork or Fiverr and ask for captions, b roll, music, graphics and jump cuts. Once you get the fancy video, *then* post.
- Do this once a week at first, then three times a week, and work your way up to once a day.

ACT 4:

ALIGNMENT

When I was at theatre school, I was often worried about coming across as gay. I was nineteen, I had lost my brother two years before, and had been wrongfully arrested for physical and sexual assault charges three months after my brother had died. This affected me in ways I'm still unravelling, but at the time the grief and subsequent shock was so acute that I developed a fear of sex and intimacy (even though I had a relationship at the time, it was full of toxicity: both my girlfriend and I were dealing with intense traumas and had no idea how to treat each other properly).

Obviously, I knew that being gay wasn't *wrong*; I certainly didn't think this of any of my gay and lesbian friends at theatre school. But as a young man desperately depressed and insecure about his masculinity (and having grown up in the '90s and 2000s, a generally homophobic time), I didn't want anyone to think I was effeminate, or weak, or anything associated with the negative stereotypes of a gay male. Also, I was an actor (not considered the manliest of professions). So I tried hard to be tough and mas-culine. I worked out like a bodybuilder, ate, drank, did drugs to excess, and sometimes got in fights on the weekend. I acted in ways that I would wake up the next day ashamed of, and then do it all again the next night.

I was accused of being overly macho by my teachers at theatre school. I was told I was "resisting the work" when I rolled my eyes at some of the more outlandish exercises we would do. I was having real trouble healing from my recent traumatic experiences, as well as figuring out who I wanted to be. I slowly realized that many of these troubles stemmed from the fact that I didn't know *why* I was at theatre school.

My classmates, by contrast, seemed to know exactly why they were there: they wanted to be actors, more than anything. I, on the other hand, was there by default. I had been an actor since the age of seven, and was decently talented enough to build a successful acting career as a child (which allowed me to graduate debt-free, and even make some investments). I always liked the work itself, too. I liked the idea of getting into a character, researching the kind of life people like them lived, imagining how different emotional experiences would affect them, or recognizing my own emotional experiences in theirs. But there was one key problem: I didn't want to be an actor *more than anything else,* and that was ultimately what made me so miserable.

Looking back now, all my efforts in school were not to be the best actor I could be — they were to prove to myself and others that I was good enough, that I was man enough, that I was cool enough. It was *all about what everybody else thought of me.* I did my best to project confidence, but inside all I wanted was love, approval, and validation of my talent from other people.

My actions, my thoughts, the things I would say, the way I felt inside — everything felt out of ALIGNMENT. As the French existentialists would describe it, the "performance of self" I was putting on lacked authenticity. Authenticity is a concept that Mark Manson, self-described existentialist and author of *The Subtle Art of Not Giving* *a F**k*, defines as "acting in the world in a way that is an accurate reflection of your feelings, beliefs, and ideas."[24]

Why am I telling you all this? Because being in Alignment is crucial if you want to be not just an effective speaker, but also a powerful one. When a speaker is *out* of Alignment, the audience can often sense it. They know the speaker doesn't really want to be here. They know the speaker is not really excited about what they're talking about, and may give up on their work when it gets hard or something better comes along. That's what my teachers at theatre school sensed about me, and they were right.

In this chapter, I'm going to share with you more stories that have shaped my understanding of Alignment — which is Act 4 in the OutLoud Method — and give you the tools you need to make sure people can always feel your excitement when you talk about what you do.

VULNERABILITY IS KEY

The introduction to this chapter was hard for me to write. There are things in there about myself and my past that I'd rather forget, and sharing them with you, the reader, is terrifying.

What if you judge me for some reason or another? What if it makes you stop reading because you look at me differently now? What if the topics I wrote about or the way I wrote about them offended you? What if you read it and then later make fun of me for these painful moments — either in person or online?

All of that is a possibility; but I'm willing to bet, like most people,

---

24 Manson, M. (n.d.). "Why I am not a Stoic." *Mark Manson.* https://markmanson.net/why-i-am-not-a-stoic

what I shared with you made you empathize rather than judge. Most people are much more comfortable once you share something about yourself, as it gives them permission to open up if there's anything heavy that *they* are carrying.

My first speaking gig after the New Orleans one (which I described in the last chapter) was in Texas, for the Dallas chapter of the same organization, EO. I had got the gig after I spoke in NOLA, and this subsequent Dallas gig led to several others that are still generating opportunities. (That's the "virtuous cycle" I mentioned in Act 3 — but that's not the point I want to focus on here.)

As I was on stage in front of forty-odd CEOs in Dallas, coaching volunteers on their public speaking and answering questions, I began to tell a story from my time in theatre school, which alluded to the insecurities about my masculinity that I wrote about in the previous section. It went a bit like this:

"During NTS [National Theatre School], I was scared to be soft or appear weak in any way when I was on stage. I was an insecure nine-teen-year-old and terrified of what people thought of me. But when I was playing the character of Ernst in the musical Cabaret *in my final year, I was somehow able to speak and move in a much more fluid, sensual and even feminine way, which suited the character perfectly. My director pointed this out, and said she thought it was the German accent I was using that allowed me to feel free. As Oscar Wilde said: 'Man is least himself when he talks in his own person. Give him a mask, and he will tell you the truth.'"*

As I was telling this story, every single audience member was listening intently. Afterward, the guy who hired me told me it was his favourite part of the workshop. "You could've heard a pin drop in there," he said. "And it was because you admitted to something so *vulnerable.*"

Admitting to fears, insecurities, self-doubt, painful experiences, and other scary secrets we usually hold close to our chest has an incredible effect in public speaking situations: it *changes the entire energy of the room,* because we've shown people something *real* about ourselves. Not something impressive — which most people think they need to do in professional situations — but something *vulnerable.* People know they can trust us because we've trusted them. *Trust* is at the heart of speaking (and living) in Alignment.

I've talked about my brother's death and its impact on me several times in my workshops or webinars. I've had participants tell me about recent deaths in their family. I've seen many people cry and share stories of abuse or assault, crimes they've committed, past addiction or mental health crises. As scary or inappropriate as this may sound to you, these moments remain memorable and important ones in my career, and were beautiful to be a part of. Many of my clients who share personal details contact me afterwards to say "thank you."

You can *feel* it when somebody becomes vulnerable in the room. It's like tunnel vision: all your thoughts quiet down, and all you can see and hear is the person talking, sharing their story. Your heart goes out to them. It can be uncomfortable, or painful, but when handled with care and professionalism, deeply vulnerable statements and stories will affect your audience in ways you can't even predict.

Learning to share the parts of your life that are painful, and even shameful, is one of the most powerful things you can do — not only as a public speaker, but also, I believe, as a leader, a colleague, a friend, a spouse, and even a stranger (whether IRL or online). I can't say it any better than the queen of speaking about vulnerability, Brené Brown, who writes in *Daring Greatly* that:

"*Vulnerability is the core, the heart, the centre, of meaningful human experiences.*"

If you share with others, they will know you, like you, trust you, and even love you. However, you must be able to share *without* these expectations: the point of sharing must be healing and helping others, which can only be done if you have healed and helped yourself a bit first. I'll let Brené have the last word:

"*Vulnerability is based on mutuality and requires boundaries and trust. It's not oversharing, it's not purging, it's not indiscriminate disclosure, and it's not celebrity-style social media information dumps. Vulnerability is about sharing our feelings and our experiences with people who have earned the right to hear them.*"[25]

'IKIGAI' – ANOTHER KEY TO ALIGNMENT

As those who know me well are aware, I've been diagnosed with anxiety and depression. I started taking medication for it only *after* I left my first start-up in China, due to a debilitating back injury that forced me to go home to recover. I found myself back in Canada staying on my mother's couch, unable to dress myself, climb stairs, or even walk for the better part of a year.

---

25 Brown, B. (2016). *Daring Greatly: How the Courage to Be Vulnerable Transforms the Way We Live, Love, Parent, and Lead.* Penguin Life.

As you can imagine, that year was rough — not least for my mum and stepdad, who had to take care of me. Because of the injury, I was even more depressed than normal. I couldn't exercise, spend time outdoors, see many friends, go on dates, or even hold down a job. I tried teaching online, but the pain medication made it too difficult to be an effective teacher, as I was constantly high on Percocet.

But there was a deeper, underlying issue that made my depression so extreme: *I had no idea what I was going to do with my life after I recovered.*

Would I go back to acting? Teaching? Would I try to make money as a musician, a long-time dream of mine? Would I go back to working in clubs and restaurants, or on construction sites (as I'd done before I left Canada to live in Spain and China), even though those weren't passions of mine? Should I go back to school? What would I study? How long could I wait to take a job? What did my lack of a coherent career path *say* about me? Why didn't I have a clear vision of what to do? What woman would want to be with such a loser? Why should I even do my physio exercises to try and get better? What use was life anyway?? Why was all of this happening to *me*?!

As you can probably sense just reading that, this cycle of thoughts — some of which you may relate to yourself — drove me crazy, and it wasn't until I went to therapy that things changed. I eventually found a therapist who practiced cognitive behavioural therapy (CBT) with me, and I started to be able to recognize my anxious and depressed thoughts for what they often are: lying voices interested in their own self-perpetuation.[26]

---

26 Charlamagne tha God's 2019 book *Shook One: How My Anxiety Plays Tricks on Me* (Atria Books) sums up this dynamic well. He also talks about how while anxiety can be helpful and motivating at times, as we progress through life it generally starts to work against us.

My main problem, I discovered, was a lack of *direction*, but in a much deeper sense: I had not yet found my *ikigai*, and as a result my attitude, demeanour, and work ethic were not inspired by any greater sense of purpose.

Ikigai is a Japanese word that is similar to the French expression *raison d'être* ("reason for being"). The Oxford English Dictionary defines it as:

"a motivating force; something or someone that gives a person a sense of purpose or a reason for living."

When I learned there was a *word* for what I had been lacking — and therefore suffering from being without — for so many years, I felt like crying. Ever since I'd realized I didn't want to be an actor, deciding what I was going to do with my life had seemed impossible. Going first to Spain to teach English, then to China to start a company, is a cool story to tell people. But what I don't often say is that I was miserable for most of that time, because I had no sense of purpose. But my *ikigai*, my reason for being, was like many of life's valuable lessons: only *after* I'd found it did I learn how to describe it.

Before we take a closer look at this concept, it should be said the version of "ikigai" we're dealing with here is a Westernized version which puts a lot more emphasis on career and money. I use this because I'm more familiar with it and I'm an outsider to Japanese culture; but I also believe that this version is more appropriate to my purpose as a business and pitch coach.

Your *ikigai* is said to lie at the centre of a Venn diagram with four overlapping circles, as per the diagram below. One circle is "what you love," another is "what you are good at," a third is "what you can be paid for," and the last is "what the world needs."

As you can see, this concept runs deeper than Western/ English-language ideas of "passion" or "mission." All four of the criteria represented in the circles above need to be met to find your *ikigai* — and when you do, the results are barely believable.

Here are some documented stats from a Japanese study of over 43,000 participants.[27] Those who answered "yes" to having *ikigai*:

- had a lower risk for cardiovascular disease,
- reported less stress,
- reported better mental health,
- and were more likely to be educated,
- married, and
- employed.

---

27 Sone, T. et al. (2008). "Sense of life worth living (*ikigai*) and mortality in Japan." *Psychosomatic Medicine, 70,* 709-715.

Referencing this study, *Psychology Today* wrote: "Said another way, 95% of respondents who reported a sense of meaning in their lives were alive seven years after the initial survey, versus about 83% of those who reported no sense of meaning in their lives."[28]

The presence or absence of a sense of meaning in one's life can extend or shorten it. That's important enough on its own as a sociological finding, but what does it tell us about public speaking? Not enough data exists on this, but it's my contention that those who have *ikigai* are much better speakers than those who don't, particularly when they're speaking *about* their *ikigai*. And it's here that *true* Alignment starts.

When I realized I could help people and make money doing something I loved and was good at, it completely changed my life. After I started OutLoud, it was like a light switch had been flipped on. Suddenly, good things started happening: I became more confident and motivated; I started prioritizing good habits like getting rest and organizing my email; I quit doing drugs and became much more productive; I developed a reputation as a coach and public speaker, which led to more and more opportunities and clients; and I met my now-wife, and was able to mature into the kind of man I never thought I could be. All of this because, I'm convinced, my life now had *meaning.*

When I get onstage to do my thing, I can win over even the most skeptical crowd and prove myself in front of more accomplished, qualified, and experienced men and women. I can do this because, deep in my heart, I *believe* in what I'm saying. I know this work helps people. I know it has value, monetarily and beyond. I know I'm good at it (although it took me a long time to feel comfortable saying that,

28 Peterson, C. (2008, September 17). "*Ikigai* and mortality." *Psychology Today.* https://www.psychologytoday.com/us/blog/the-good-life/200809/ikigai-and-mortality

and even now I feel like a douchebag writing it). And I truly *love* it.

Me standing onstage now, versus me before finding my *ikigai*, is completely different. You can see and hear it whenever I talk.

My assumption, if you're reading a book like this, is that you've already found your *ikigai,* or at least have a general sense of what you want to do for a living. If not, there are some great articles, podcasts, and books about how to find your *ikigai*; here, though, I'm just going to give you a writing exercise to help you *talk* about your *ikigai* in a way that will make audiences respond to and respect you. Passion is contagious, and when you remind yourself *why* you love what you do, and make an effort to show it, the people listening to you will get excited.

So, write down the answers to the questions below, either now or later. Take your time with them — maybe even try closing your eyes and breathing deeply three or four times before getting started, as this will help get you into a "visualization" frame of mind. It may seem hokey, but it really helps!

1. What moments in your childhood — happy, sad, or otherwise — do you think had an impact on *why you do the work you do today?* Write these out in as much detail as possible, and look for connections between then and now.
2. In what ways does your work suit your personality? What traits do you have that are perfect for what you do, and why?
3. What's the nicest thing a client, customer, partner, manager, or colleague has ever said to you about what you do? How many can you think of? What feelings does writing all them down bring up?
4. What would the world be like if what you do *didn't exist?* How would things be worse, and for whom? Why does your work

really matter? Put down one or two real stories of clients or people you've helped out, and how they were suffering beforehand.

5. Forget how much money you *wish* you were making for a second: what does your current income allow you to buy that you need and love? Write one thing you've bought today, this week, this month, and this year that you're grateful for.

6. What would you be doing if not what you do now? Would you be happier?

So far in this chapter I've talked a lot about authenticity and vulnerability and life's purpose. I realize these things might not seem directly related to your speaking skills, but I hope that I've managed to convey to you that you must be vulnerable, authentic, and passionate to be a truly successful and appealing speaker. And if you're speaking about a career that is truly your calling, you will inevitably speak with greater appeal and authenticity.

In other words, a lot of the work to make the way you speak look and feel right on the outside is actually done on the *inside*. For the rest of this chapter, we're going to look at how to ensure that the outside (how you look and sound) is Aligned with your authentic inside (how you feel), so that your audience can see how great you truly are.

"CONGRUENCE": THE FORGOTTEN LESSON OF DR. MEHRABIAN

Albert Mehrabian was born in Iran in 1939. He moved to the US to study engineering at MIT, but felt called to psychology and switched career paths, ultimately becoming a successful professor and researcher — and never suspecting that, one day, he would become one of the most widely misquoted and misunderstood researchers in the history of business seminars.

You have probably heard Mehrabian's name because of the "7-38-55 rule," which is plastered all over shoddily made graphics on PowerPoint and social media by gullible communication coaches (including me early in my career, I'm embarrassed to say) to illustrate a cool-sounding but completely false fact. It usually goes something like this:

"*Communication is:*

- *7% words*
- *38% tone of voice*
- *55% facial expression*"

Now, while this formula may help shift our focus to our tone of voice and Facial Expression — which is extremely important — those percentages are ridiculous. Do you honestly believe that we lose *93%* of a message when we read something via email, versus hearing it while face to face? Of course not — and, as Dr. Mehrabian himself points out,[29] the study that the rule derived from pertained only to people talking about their feelings and emotions, and he categorically states that applying the rule in any other context is a mistake.

However, that hasn't stopped communication coaches all over the world from teaching it as a "public speaking rule." But it's a truly unfortunate error, not only because it's wrong, but also because

---

29 Mehrabian, A. (1981). "Silent messages: A wealth of information about nonverbal communication (body language)." *Personality & Emotion Tests & Software: Psychological Books & Articles of Popular Interest.* http://www.kaaj.com/psych/smorder.html

it overshadows another concept that Dr. Mehrabian formulated, which I think is his most valuable contribution to the science of interpersonal communication: *congruence.*

Congruence means the three elements in the often erroneously applied 7-38-55 rule:

- words
- tone of voice
- facial expression

need to support each other to create effective, meaningful communication.[30]

I'll take it a step further:

In order to communicate at your highest level (to be in ALIGNMENT), your thoughts, feelings, beliefs, words, body, face and voice all need to tell the same story.

This is what alignment looks like: someone speaking from the heart, passionate, engaged, and certain about what they truly believe in, which you can *see, hear,* and *feel* in every word.

Now, if you haven't found your *ikigai*, then this will be hard for you to do. That's why so few junior members of companies are effective presenters: because they haven't found their true career path yet, and the subject matter often bores them to death. But if you *have* found your *ikigai*, or something close to it, there are ways you can *practise getting into Alignment.* We'll look at these next.

---

30 Mehrabian, ibid.

START WITH WHY

If you're a fan of public speaking as an art form, you've probably heard of Simon Sinek. He's as close as you get to a star in this field, and in my opinion deserves the recognition he gets as a performer because of how passionately he speaks and how he's able to take simple truths about speaking and leadership and make them profound, actionable, and accessible.

His book *Start With Why* is a phenomenal resource for people learning to tell their story, and he illustrates a powerful *restructuring* of the way we tell stories. Let me explain.

When we give our "elevator pitch" for our work or business, many of us start with WHAT we do, saying something like this:

"Hi, my name is Will, and I run a public speaking coaching company called OutLoud Speakers School. We help entrepreneurs and executives tell powerful stories to grow their business. We run coaching courses for groups and individuals online to improve their speaking and storytelling skills."

Not a bad summary: it's clear, understandable, and defines *who* we help plus *how* we help them. But what about the *why*?

Consider this version of the same elevator pitch:

"I started acting at the age of seven. I loved it, but I was always terrified about what other people thought of me. When I quit acting, I found entrepreneurship, and I realized my experience and training could help other founders speak with confidence and clarity.

"My name is Will, and I run a training company called OutLoud

Speakers School. We help entrepreneurs and executives tell powerful stories to grow their business."

Which version do you think would draw you in more effectively as an opener to a pitch or presentation? Which one is more memorable? Which helps you understand me more as a person and business owner?

I'm willing to bet you'd agree with me that it's the second one. Not just because we started with a story (as we talked about in Act 2: Articulation), but because we started with WHY. The reason I started my business, why it's so personal for me, why I won't just quit and do something else, why I'm committed to my clients and why they can trust me to help them with what they're going through — all of it is right there in the very beginning.

All of that information is crucial to convey to your audience, especially if they're potential customers or investors. If you can demonstrate a knowledge of and commitment to the people you help — i.e., the people in your target market — by explaining why you are so passionate about helping them, then they will be much more likely to buy into you.

You can apply this START WITH WHY rule to any piece of content or presentation. Instead of just writing down the information you feel like you need to convey, such as the "what, when, where, who" and "how," first ask yourself a series of "why" questions, such as:

1. Why did you start this business/career in the first place?
2. Why does this thing you are proposing (your business, your recommendation, your method, etc.) *need* to exist?
3. Why should the audience care? That is, what do *they* want? Once you have an answer for that, ask yourself why do they

want *that*? And why *that*, and *that*? Keep going until you get to something that touches on the Big 5 Human Concerns (time, money, health, relationships, and/or emotional wellbeing).

4. Why are YOU the person who can help them get this thing they want?

5. Why do YOU care so much about this topic?

6. Why is NOW the right time for this thing?

7. And finally, after pretty much every sentence you write, ask yourself: Do I BELIEVE what I just wrote? Am I being honest with myself and my audience? Am I being as *true to what I feel* as I can, without oversharing or self-sabotaging, to provide the audience with a real sense of WHY we're all here, together, in this moment, listening to me speak?

When you know WHY you do your work and why the audience *needs to hear about it* — and you remind yourself of this in specific, emotionally rich terms when you're writing or performing a pitch or presentation — then you break through the boring topsoil of normal, corporate, surface-level speech and get to the *roots* of what we all truly care about. When you talk like this, not only do people like you, but they will *love* you for opening the door to real, honest conversation. It feels exciting, and fresh, and is extremely important.

The more of us who do this, the more honest and empathetic the overall climate and culture becomes. Many of us desperately want to speak this openly, honestly, and passionately, but we're afraid of

- name-calling,
- judgment,
- being dismissed,
- trying and failing to win over an audience,

- losing status,
- feeling awkward or out of character,

or any of the other common fears we've discussed throughout this book.

Be the example for the people around you. Speak with passion, confidence, and clarity about the things you believe in, and let your thoughts, beliefs, words, voice, face and body language match, be in *congruence*, so you can show the world what it's like to be in Alignment. The people who matter will love you for it.

THE 6-DIMENSION MODEL OF NATIONAL CULTURE

Okay, so now you're ready to jump on stage or in front of the camera and start demonstrating your Alignment all over the world! All you need to do is be vulnerable, talk about your *ikigai*, start with WHY when you share your presentation, and all will be well, right?

Not quite. There's another factor to take into consideration when we talk about Alignment — your audience.

I talked earlier about how my teachers in theatre school picked up on the fact that I was out of Alignment — that I didn't really want to be an actor above all else. Well, there's more to that story. They also believed they sensed that about some of the other students, but in those cases they were wrong: these classmates of mine are now very successful and dedicated actors. I believe that one of the reasons my teachers made these errors of judgment is because miscommunication can happen when the *way* people talk about what they love doesn't *seem genuine* (which is an example of being out of Alignment) — but sometimes, a speaker can come across as not being genuine because of a *cultural divide*.

This is what we're going to talk about now: how to adapt your speech and performance so that you can cross that cultural divide when speaking to international audiences. It's not about changing who you *are*, it's about Aligning with the culture of the audience you're talking to.

Let's start with an example from my own experience. I remember being in Mexico doing a keynote workshop for an international group of executives. While I was eating dinner with some of the participants, two of the German members told me, in typically blunt Northern European fashion: "We liked your workshop, but all of this crazy 'rah-rah' stuff, it will never work in Germany." They were referring to all the warm-ups and techniques I had shown them (which I detailed in Act 1: Awareness), and the enthusiasm with which I pumped up the crowd.

I laughed, because I knew immediately what they meant. Germans are generally much more reserved than Americans, who made up most of the attendees at that workshop, as well as most of my clients up to that point. Germans tend to care much less for loudness and goofiness than people from the US, especially in professional situations.

This isn't simply a stereotype. I've been to Germany, lived and worked with many Germans during my time in Spain, and coached dozens of them over the years, but the anecdotal evidence I can provide for that claim is backed up by real scientific data. Believe it or not, there are ways some sociologists measure how certain behaviours are manifested more or less strongly in certain cultures, and the most compelling method I've come across is Geert Hofstede's 6-dimension model of national culture.

I discovered Hofstede's work after reading Malcolm Gladwell's *Outliers*, in which he describes how the investigation of the crash of Korean Air Cargo Flight 8509 in 1999 indicated how Korean communication habits may have contributed to the deadly accident. "Korean Air had more plane crashes than almost any other airline in the world for a period at the end of the 1990s," Gladwell told *Fortune* just after the book came out. "What they were struggling with was a cultural legacy, that Korean culture is hierarchical. You are obliged to be deferential toward your elders and superiors in a way that would be unimaginable in the US."[31]

The idea of culture affecting communication fascinated me, especially as someone who hadn't travelled much at the time.[32] When I eventually moved to China to start my first company, one of my responsibilities as co-founder was to research "cross-cultural training": ways to study and teach about other cultures for both Western and Chinese businesspeople looking to impress colleagues and clients from abroad. Remembering Gladwell's use of the term "Power Distance" — which, I thought, seemed like it could be the dynamic at play in the confusion between Chinese and Western etiquette — I began digging deeper into the literature on this subject.

This is when I first encountered Hofstede's 6 dimensions of national culture, a framework that measures almost every country on Earth along six "personality traits" — or, as Hofstede puts it, "six

---

31 Ohlheiser, A. (2013, July 10). "Malcolm Gladwell's cockpit culture theory and the Asiana crash." *The Atlantic*. https://www.theatlantic.com/national/archive/2013/07/malcolm-gladwells-cockpit-culture-theory-everywhere-after-asiana-crash/313442/

32 It should be said that there is a great counter-argument to Gladwell's theory written by a Korean blogger. T.K. (2013). "Culturalism, Gladwell, and airplane crashes." *Ask a Korean!* http://askakorean.blogspot.com/2013/07/culturalism-gladwell-and-airplane.html

basic issues that society needs to come to terms with in order to organize itself."[33] These six "issues" are:

1. Power Distance
2. Individualism vs. Collectivism
3. Masculinity vs. Femininity
4. Uncertainty Avoidance
5. Long-term vs. Short-term Orientation
6. Indulgence vs. Restraint

Now, for my work as a speaking coach, I believe that dimensions 3, 4 and 5 are mostly irrelevant to communication. So let's take those out of the equation (if you'd like to learn more about the full set you can go to Hofstede's website, which is cited in the footnotes), and simplify the list as follows:

1. Power Distance
2. Individualism vs. Collectivism
3. Indulgence vs. Restraint

Let's look at each of these, one by one.

Power Distance

Hofstede defines Power Distance as, "the extent to which the less powerful members of organizations and institutions... accept and expect that power is distributed unequally."[34] Or, in layman's terms:

33 Hofstede, G. (n.d.). "The 6-D model of national culture." *Geert Hofstede*. https://geerthof-stede.com/culture-geert-hofstede-gert-jan-hofstede/6d-model-of-national-culture/

34 "The 6 dimensions of national culture." (n.d.). *Hofstede Insights*. https://www.hofst-ede-insights.com/models/national-culture/

how comfortable are "inferiors" with acknowledging their "inferiority" in any given country? In your society, do people usually think it is more important to teach children RESPECT or INDEPENDENCE? Do employees in your country call their bosses by respectful titles or first names? Are people with more money or political power considered *better* than others, or not?

All these values about how *equal* citizens believe their society should be constitute a country's Power Distance score, which is charted on a scale of 0 to 100. A score of 100 indicates a dominant mentality of "some people are just better than others," while a 0 indicates that the prevailing sentiment is "everyone is exactly equal."

To illustrate this, according to Hofstede China's Power Distance score is 60, while Canada's is 39. This means that, in general, those who live in China are more comfortable with the idea of unequal power between individuals — especially in institutions and organizations, as well as in family life — while Canadians are generally more egalitarian. (To me, this contrast is made even more fascinating by way of the fact that China is ostensibly a communist country, where, theoretically, all should be considered equal — but that's a whole other conversation!)

I can offer my own experience to support that rating: while living in Hangzhou, I observed a far stricter hierarchy than I was used to seeing in Canada. Children were more respectful to their parents, grandparents and schoolteachers; employees were often treated like servants by their bosses; and many middle-class households actually *had* servants, or *"ayis,"* as they were called.

It's important to note, though, that none of the ratings on Hofstede's Power Distance scale carry a value judgment. Being higher or lower does not make a culture better or worse: it just gives us insight into how certain behaviours are likely to be *perceived* when we meet people from different countries. And knowing this can be extremely useful for *respectful and powerful communication.*

In higher Power Distance countries like China, Egypt, or the Philippines, public speakers can be observed:

- avoiding eye contact,
- speaking softly, and
- using self-deprecating language

in order to appear respectful and deferential to their audience. By contrast, in lower Power Distance countries like Canada and the US, good speakers tend to do the opposite, by:

- speaking loudly,
- making eye contact to show confidence, and
- using strong language to speak about their ideas.

Here, there is not as much fear of offending an audience by suggesting that you are equal to or "above" them. Thus, a speaker's words, tone, and choice of language changes accordingly.

Now, how do the other two dimensions factor in to communication?

Individualism vs. Collectivism

As Hofstede puts it, individualism is "the extent to which people feel independent, as opposed to being interdependent as members of a larger whole." It is not necessarily egoism, but rather a society where "individual choices and decisions are expected." Collectivism, meanwhile, means "knowing one's place in life, which is determined socially."[35]

---

35 Ibid.

To give some examples from Hofstede's ratings, China, a highly collectivist country, is a 20 (out of 100) on the Individualism scale. The US — perhaps unsurprisingly to anyone familiar with American culture — is a whopping 91. Canada is 80, slightly less than our southern neighbours but still very individualistic. Guatemala, meanwhile, is the most collectivist country in the world, with a 6 in Individualism: according to Hofstede, "communication [here] is indirect and the harmony of the group has to be maintained; open conflicts are avoided."[36]

As you can see, this dimension is very relevant to speaking styles. Also, there is a lot of overlap between Individualism and Power Distance in how they manifest themselves in communication. Collectivist public speakers (such as those from Guatemala or China) trying to impress a like-minded audience usually:

- avoid confrontational language (verbal and non-verbal),
- choose commonly accepted words and ideas, and
- position themselves as "one of the audience."

Whereas, if they were seeking to impress an audience of Individualists (like Americans), they would do better to:

- highlight their uniqueness,
- be bold and even aggressive about challenging the audience, and
- show initiative and innovation.

---

36 "Country Comparison: Guatemala." (n.d.). *Hofstede Insights*. https://www.hofstede-insights.com/country-comparison/guatemala/

Again, neither style is necessarily better than the other, but we can see how speaking to an audience of either all Collectivists or all Individualists might require a slightly different touch.

Indulgence vs. Restraint

This one is fascinating. Hofstede defines the indulgence–restraint dynamic as "the extent to which people try to control their desires and impulses,"[37] and this has several ramifications for speech.

Indulgent cultures, like those of Canada and the US, have relatively weak control over their desires and impulses, and don't think that curbing them is important. They value experience and pleasure, and are generally more optimistic and fun-seeking.

In a public speaking situation, we can see this trait manifested through:

- high vocal inflection and emotional tone,
- bigger gestures and movements, and
- emotive facial expressions, like smiling or frowning.

On the other end of the spectrum, speakers who hail from a culture where Restraint is dominant evince this through:

- a calm, even monotonous tone of voice,
- minimalistic body language, and
- less overt emotional expression.

So, when we put all this information together, we can now cobble together a little "cheat sheet" for how to be a good speaker

---

37 "The 6 dimensions of national culture." *Hofstede Insights.*

in various regions. A good speaker in North American terms will be one who is LOUD, CONFIDENT, EXPRESSIVE and EMOTIONAL. By contrast, good speakers in Asia (or Guatemala) will most often be characterized by being CALM, QUIET, HUMBLE and CONTAINED.

Of course, all of these are just generalizations. You yourself may not fit into the designated cultural norm of your country, or even agree that such a norm exists. However, I've helped thousands of clients and students from all over the world gain insights into Canadian and American culture — especially around speaking and communication — and so I encourage you to keep an open mind, do some further reading, and reflect on how these concepts could help you in your journey to become a better public speaker. Remember, the first Act is AWARENESS, and only by first being *aware* can we gather all the information and wisdom we need to get into ALIGNMENT.

Let's summarize what we've covered in this chapter,

SUMMARY

- Sharing something vulnerable, with care and thought, changes the energy of the room, and gets people empathizing and connecting with you; it even frees them up to be vulnerable themselves.
- Vulnerability should be shared for its own sake, not for pity, attention or manipulation.
- People who have *ikigai* tend to live longer and are healthier, happier and more productive. Even if you've found yours, work to remind yourself and SHOW it in your face, hands, body, voice and WORDS!

- The Mehrabian "7-38-55 rule" is rubbish, but his term *congru-ence* (i.e., face, tone, and words all matching) is important for building *trust* with your audience.
- To be a great speaker, your thoughts, feelings, beliefs, words, hands, face, body and voice should all be TELLING THE SAME STORY.
- Starting with WHY can help to remind yourself, and then tell the audience, what is IMPORTANT and AT STAKE when you talk about your business and why you're passionate about it.
- Geert Hofstede's 6-dimensional model of national culture pro-vides valuable insights into different cultural communication styles, including the three most important dimensions that, I believe, affect communication: Power Distance, Individualism vs. Collectivism, and Indulgence vs. Restraint.

You're now almost ready. We've covered many of the essential ingredients for powerful presentations, successful speeches, and viral videos. Our next chapter, Act 5: Automation, is about putting it all together, and developing habits that will last a lifetime.

ACT 5:

AUTOMATION

As an entrepreneur, I've often felt like an impostor — for that matter, I've even felt the same about simply being an adult. The only reason I feel confident saying "I am an actor" is because I grew up doing it professionally and trained at a top school. I can also say quite confidently that my personality type is in line with that of the stereotypical actor: I'm loud and extroverted, I like being the centre of attention, I'm curious and overly analytical about people, and I have a deep, desperate, and often unfortunate desire to be liked by everyone. In combination with the 20,000+ hours I've spent working on my craft as an actor, my natural personality gives me an advantage over other business owners, as I'm able to be expressive, clear, engaging, personable, and memorable as a speaker and communicator.

However, another trait I have that seems common among actors is a *lack of organizational skills*. Many of us artists spend much of our time with our heads in the clouds, thinking of stories and characters and emotions, and we're usually far more interested in feelings than in facts and figures. This was a disadvantage when I started my business, as I had to work twice as hard to learn certain skills: how to balance a budget, how to organize my schedule, how to follow through with potential clients, and how to set up systems that will do these things *automatically* so I can stay on top of everything. I became obsessed with figuring out how to optimize my work week by *automating* as many tasks as I could. And then I realized that, in the same way we build habits in order to be more productive or healthier, to improve a skill or master a second language, we need to build habits to improve our speaking skills.

As James Clear, author of *Atomic Habits*, says: "You don't rise to the level of your goals; you fall to the level of your systems."[38] You can dream of delivering viral TED Talks and big-stage keynotes, but if you don't develop the right habits, you'll never get there. Let's dive in to Act 5: Automation and see how you can use *habits* — the process of making behaviours automatic — to help you become the best speaker you can be.

THE VALUE OF *RÉPÉTITION*

When I decided to record my first musical album, thinking about going into the studio made me panic. I'd never taken guitar lessons, and I wanted the guitar to sound professional, or at least passable, on the record. But I had no budget to hire a professional studio guitarist, so it was up to me to do it. I found a local guitar teacher from a flyer on a lamp post, and started taking "fingerstyle" lessons.

Fingerstyle is a way of picking the guitar using (you guessed it) your fingers, rather than a pick. It sounds magical when done well: it's as though several people are playing at once, due to the variations from high and low notes plucked by the thumb and fingers on your right hand. There are infinite patterns, and every time you

---

38 Clear, J. (2021). *Atomic Habits: Tiny Changes, Remarkable Results — An Easy & Proven Way to Build Good Habits & Break Bad Ones*. CELA.

learn a new one it takes a lot of time and precise practice to get your fingers to accomplish these micro-acrobatics.

Now, I've never been good at practising, or studying, or *working*, for that matter. I have a terrible time concentrating, and I tend to move on as soon as I can do something decently rather than sticking around to perfect it. But this guitar teacher said something very important to me, which I like to repeat to my clients today: "My job is to teach you how to teach yourself."

Rather than teach me how to play guitar, he taught me how to learn a new skill: how to break a practice session down into sections, and what to look for in my own playing. He gave me instruction, but his focus was on teaching me how to get better at home by myself. This is exactly what I now want to do for my clients: I don't want them to have to come back to me every week for the rest of their lives, I want them to learn enough from me that they can improve for the rest of their lives *on their own*. That's why Act 5: Automation, is all about BECOMING *YOUR OWN COACH*.

At theatre school in Montréal, our teachers told us again and again that the French word for "rehearsal" is *répétition,* or, in English, "repetition" (obviously). The French term speaks to the belief that, in order to be ready for opening night, you have to rehearse again and again and again until your performance is embedded in your mind and body and you can't get it wrong.

Another way to say this is "shedding," a term I heard from an actor friend of mine who was a skilled fingerstyle guitar player. It comes from the musician's word "woodshedding," which means going to a remote place (like a shed) where no one can hear you and practising until you can play a difficult passage, song, or even technique flawlessly.

This is what I needed to do to get better at guitar and be able to play on my own record. I stopped taking lessons with the fingerstyle teacher after only two months, because by then I knew how to learn and practise by myself. Instead, I started "shedding": playing difficult songs and fingerstyle patterns over and over, learning new techniques and practising them even after my sore hand and bored brain told me to give up. I rehearsed my own fingerstyle compositions and strumming patterns until I felt confident enough to record my album in the studio and play my own guitar.

I'm far from a virtuoso, but to this day, when I listen to that album, I feel immensely happy that I put in the work to play my own guitar, and now can perform in front of crowds without feeling like an impostor. Some of this confidence (or at least lack of panic) came from a shift in mindset, some from getting more performance experience, but much of it came from shedding, rehearsal, and *répétition*.

HOW TO PRACTISE

You may know the old joke: "How do you get to Carnegie Hall? Practice, practice, practice." Or, in Malcolm Gladwell's parlance, it's called "the 10,000-hour rule." However you want to phrase it, we all know we need to dedicate time, attention, and effort to a skill in order to master it. But, like any skill, there are right ways and wrong ways to practise public speaking and communication — and believe me, I see a lot of them.

I've had clients tell me they were instructed to hold a "pretend beach ball" so that their hands were "always in the right position"; but when they did so they looked robotic and stiff as they spoke, with no natural movement in their arms. I've seen speaking coaches silently stare at their audience for 30 seconds, until the whole room was deeply uncomfortable, and then declare that this was how you "build rapport" (okay, sure...). And even brilliant coaches like Carmine Gallo, author of *Talk Like TED*,[39] tell their clients and readers to "practise relentlessly" without necessarily telling them HOW to practise. For instance, should I be sitting in a chair when I practise, or standing up? Do I walk around? Do I say it the same way each time? Should I be louder or softer, slower or faster, more or less expressive? How do I know? Should I ask a friend? Should I film myself and watch it back? What should they or I be listening for?

Practise relentlessly, yes. Rehearsal = *répétition*, yes. But HOW you rehearse is just as important as HOW OFTEN, and it can go really wrong if you are ingraining bad habits by the constant repetition of unhelpful techniques or unconscious tics.

So, in this chapter I'm going to show you HOW to rehearse so that you can automate the *right* techniques and avoid automating the *wrong* ones.

BEWARE OF DAILY JARGON FATIGUE

If you're alone right now, do me a favour: I'd like you to say your own name out loud. Go on, don't be shy.

Now that you've done it, tell me: did you say your name *slowly, clearly, loudly* and with *emotional expression?*

Probably not, right? Unless you have a name that people constantly mishear, meaning you've had to *teach* people how to say your name for your whole life, chances are you *mumble your own*

---

39 Gallo, C. (2022). *Talk Like Ted: The 9 Public Speaking Secrets of the World's Top Minds*. Pan Books.

name whenever you say it. Almost every single one of my clients does this, and so do I very often. Why do you think this is?

A concept that helps explain this phenomenon is what linguist Steven Pinker calls "the curse of knowledge." This refers to the difficulty humans encounter when we assume, mostly unconsciously, that everyone else has the same information in their brains that we do. Essentially, *the more you know about something, the worse you are at explaining it.*

We think everyone knows our jargon or acronyms, that our specific knowledge is common knowledge, and that our implications are clear without being spelled out. In a fantastic lecture you can find on YouTube called "The Sense of Style,"[40] Pinker illustrates the problem through the example of a common scientific study that was made famous by Mark Haddon's novel *The Curious Incident of the Dog in the Night-Time.* It goes something like this:

Children are shown a box of candy, and then asked what's inside. They usually reply (correctly) "candy," after which the scientists empty the candy out and replace them with pencils. When asked again, the children mostly respond that "pencils" are now inside the candy box (also correct). The interesting part comes when the scientists ask the children what other kids who walk into the room will think is inside the candy box now. Many children will say "pencils" instead of "candy" (even though the other kids couldn't possibly know there would be pencils in the candy box), because they cannot imagine that others do not have the same information they do.

---

40 https://www.youtube.com/watch?v=pn87EqoBb14&t=5s&ab_channel=Psycho-logicalScience

While our tendency to this kind of spontaneous reaction recedes as we grow up, it stays with us into our adulthood in the form of *unclear communication*. Pinker's lecture is focused on bad writing, but the same holds true of bad speaking. When communicating, if we don't remember that *we are the only ones who know what we know*, we are falling prey to the curse of knowledge.

This is why we often mumble or mutter our own name: we know it so deeply and so well that we forget that others could be hearing it for the first time. (This is especially the case if we're speaking in a foreign country.) Therefore, we often say our name with almost no effort or emphasis, making it come out muddy or even inaudible.

The other variable that makes us mumble, in my opinion, is one of the strongest human impulses: laziness. This is a prime factor in how the pronunciation of English and other languages changes over time, as linguist John McWhorter explains in his book *The Language Hoax*. Like the brain and other parts of the body, the human mouth is constantly looking for more efficient ways to do the same activities. So, over time, we shorten vowels and drop consonants, until this mangled pronunciation becomes the new norm.

If you've ever spoken Spanish to Cubans, you'll know how they often drop the letter "s" out of every word and still somehow communicate perfectly. To take an example from English, the word "nevew" eventually became "nephew," because the "f" sound was easier to make coming out of the "short e" sound than that of a "v": the "v" requires more vibration, and possibly even the lower lip receding behind the top teeth, whereas the "f" just requires a little bit of contact between the lip and teeth and a bit of aspiration (i.e., breathing in).

This lingual laziness, plus the curse of knowledge, negatively affects the way we say the most commonly used words in our vocabulary. The words we say the most *often*, some of which are the most *important,* we tend to *underemphasize,* basically mumbling them under our breath at top speed, because our mouths and brains are so sick of saying them and are so familiar with their meaning that we don't realize how unclear we're being when we try to communicate them to others.

I call these common and important phrases Daily Jargon, which 99% of people (note: not a real stat ☺) consistently underemphasize due to Daily Jargon Fatigue (or DJF). These phrases include such vital information as:

- your name
- the name of your company
- your job title
- common words, phrases and expressions in your field, company or job description
- common acronyms in your field, company or job description
- famous people or events that others may not know
- large "noun group" phrases ("Canadian, family-owned, farm-to-table restaurants")
- long, buzzword-filled business-y phrases (e.g., "We need to incentivize our end users to iterate different optionalities and evangelize for our brand." Shoot me.)

All of these can be potential times when your Daily Jargon Fatigue comes out. Consider the following paragraph (a version of my elevator pitch for OutLoud):

"Hi, my name is Will Greenblatt, and I'm the CEO and co-founder of OutLoud Speakers School. We help entrepreneurs and organizations like Google, Wayfair, and Ericsson with public speaking,

communication and storytelling skills to increase the ROI of their customer- and stakeholder-facing presentations."

Let's pretend for the moment that the above is perfectly written (even though it's not), and for whatever reason we can't change it; those are the words we're going with. Which words do you think are in danger of Daily Jargon Fatigue?

If you said:

- *Will Greenblatt,*
- *CEO,*
- *co-founder,*
- *OutLoud Speakers School,*
- *entrepreneurs,*
- *organizations,*
- *Google, Wayfair, Ericsson,*
- *public speaking, communication, storytelling skills,*
- *ROI,* and
- *customer- and stakeholder-facing presentations,*

you're absolutely right!

Think about how *crucial* those words are — these are precisely the words the audience needs to hear the most. My name; my company name; our target market; well-known clients; the content of our training program; the benefits to our customers! If anything, I should be *overemphasizing* these words.

This is where Automation comes in, as well as another important OutLoud principle, the first half of which I mentioned back in Act 1: Awareness: "Exaggerate in rehearsal, *especially when working against current habits you want to change."*

Because we've all been suffering from Daily Jargon Fatigue for 10, 20, or 30 years (or more), these habits are deeply ingrained, or *automated.* We therefore require a strict routine to counteract this habit and re-automate a new, more helpful behaviour. Here's an exercise you can use EVERY TIME YOU HAVE A PRESENTATION, once you've written or received your script or presenter notes,

1. **Bold**, <u>underline</u>, *italicize*, or write in ALL CAPS the Daily Jargon words in your script or notes (whatever method will help you remember to emphasize them).
2. Read your text out loud, saying each highlighted word LOUDER, CLEARER and SLOWER than feels normal (for EMPHASIS).
3. Repeat this three times.

Let's see how this look would look on paper, using the elevator pitch we just looked at, with the Daily Jargon words in ALL CAPS:

"Hi, my name is WILL GREENBLATT, and I'm the CEO and CO-FOUNDER of OUTLOUD SPEAKERS SCHOOL. We help ENTREPRE- NEURS and ORGANIZATIONS like GOOGLE, WAYFAIR, and ERICSSON with PUBLIC SPEAKING, COMMUNICATION and STORYTELLING SKILLS to increase the ROI of their CUSTOMER- AND STAKEHOLD- ER-FACING SALES CONVERSATIONS." [41]

This is especially important if you have to give the same spiel over and over again. To get into the habit of emphasizing your Daily Jargon and work against the years of DJF, do the above exercise

---

[41] You may need to use punctuation to remind you to *separate* each letter of the acronyms while speaking (which helps the audience understand better), so you could write them out as "C. E. O." or "C, E, O," etc.

with your script once a day, EXAGGERATING the Volume, Clarity, and slow Pace of your highlighted words. Film yourself at least once or twice and watch it back to see if you REALLY went slow/clear/loud enough. If you don't have a pitch that you tend to say all the time, make sure you rehearse this way every time you prepare for a new presentation or meeting.

To summarize:

- Write out your script.
- Highlight the Daily Jargon Fatigue words with **bold**, ALL CAPS, etc.
- Read it out loud.
- Emphasize the DJF words (extra slow, loud, and clear).
- Do this three times in a row.

This is a perfect exercise to start to practise what it feels like to *automate* good speaking skills. When you do this every day, you'll start to feel the results both internally and in the reactions of your audience: raised eyebrows, smiles, head nods and rapt attention.

Again, your Daily Jargon tends to be your most important vocabulary — you want people to HEAR and REMEMBER these words, and they'll do that if you speak them with emphasis and confidence, as if to say:

"This is my *name* and the name of my *company*: you're gonna want to **remember this**."

YOUR TOOLKIT -
THE TOP 10 SPEAKING EXERCISES

Quick question: How many times do you usually rehearse your presentation or pitch out loud before delivering it?

Often, clients will tell me they only practise something about two or three times before performing it. Sometimes, people tell me they *never* rehearse: they just feverishly edit the text and slides until the last minute, then go up there and present this material, out loud, for the very first time.

I think this is insane. We're not talking about the 60-second videos I told you to make in Act 3: Action — those are a form of practice for your important public speaking events like pitches and presentations, which are one-off performances that require *repetitive, simulative preparation* to be successful.

How the hell could you do anything well after only a couple of half-hearted practice runs at it? Imagine you had to sing a song, or do a dance, or perform a complicated yoga or martial arts routine in public with only three rehearsals beforehand, without even fully going through the motions? How likely would that be to go well?

The problem is that we've all been talking since we were around two years old, and that gives us the false sense that we don't need to practise for a speech as much as we would when performing a skill like playing guitar or breakdancing.

But the difference between *talking* and *public speaking* is like the difference between walking and playing soccer. There is so much more to think about than just making coherent sounds with your mouth. You need to:

- be loud enough, but not too loud;
- be clear, but not patronizingly so;
- emphasize key words, but the right ones and not too many;
- pause after big ideas to let them land;
- keep your energy till the end of the sentence so the final words aren't lost;
- make eye contact with your audience when you can;
- remember to breathe deeply;
- smile, use your hands and engage your eyebrows;
- remind yourself of the *emotional reality* of your words;
- ignore distractions like buzzing phones, outside noises, people seeming bored, etc.,

as well a whole host of other things, not even including technical considerations like using microphones, projecting a slide deck, or navigating Zoom.

Just because you've walked your whole life, you wouldn't suddenly think you could play soccer at a high level and compete. You know it requires practice. So, to *speak in public* at a high level, we need to practise our public speaking, and practise a lot.

However, simply reading your text out loud over and over is not going to cut it. Lionel Messi didn't become a soccer star just by playing lots of games: he needed to do specific training exercises that helped him improve. And just like soccer players need to practise passing drills, *and* work on specific gameplay scenarios like penalty kicks, *and* do cardio and stretching, we need to do lots of different "acting exercises" to improve our stamina, strength, agility, and awareness as speakers.

Luckily, I have tons of these exercises that I and thousands of other actors, as well as over 4,500 of OutLoud's clients, use to develop razor-sharp speaking skills and connect with their audience on an emotional level. Some of them are theatre-school classics; some of them I've invented; all of them work.

In the next section, I'm going to give you ten of the absolute best training exercises for improving your speaking skills. Then, in the next chapter, I'm going to show you how to make a Weekly Training Routine to commit to for the next 30 days, that will TRANSFORM your speaking skills, guaranteed, or you can email me hate messages and post angry things on my Google page or social media (@willgreenblatt).

This Weekly Training Routine will combine the things we've learned so far in this book from Acts 1 through 5, plus drills from the speaking exercises below and self-care activities like yoga, meditation, journaling, and others.

Ready? Let's dive into the TOP TEN SPEAKING EXERCISES.

1. Exaggerate a Speech Setting

Once you know your *habitual* Speech Settings (Volume, Pitch, Pace, Clarity, Inflection, Physical Expression and Facial Expression, each scored on a scale of 1 to 10) and you've identified a Setting you want to work on, read your script all the way through, EXAGGERATING that Setting *past* where you think it should be. For example, if you've been told you tend to mumble, you'd want to work on Clarity. But instead of trying for a 7 for Clarity, practise instead at a 10! Exaggerate the AB-SO-LUTE *SHIT* out of each word.

This is not the way you'd actually speak in a presentation, but this exercise will strengthen your mouth muscles, train you to have clear and sharp diction, and give you a sense of how clearly you can speak at the upper range. This makes it easier to get to a more natural, but still much clearer speaking style. You can apply this exercise to any Setting: e.g., if you worry that you speak in a mono-tone, practise a 10 in Inflection; if you think you speak way too fast, practise at a 1 for Pace, etc.

2. Explain it to your five-year-old or deaf grandma

If I have a hard time understanding the pitch or presentation during a coaching session, I often ask the client if they have any especially old or young people in their family, to which they almost always say yes. I then tell them to explain their content to their five-year-old niece, or their ninety-year-old, hard-of-hearing grandma. This forces them to do two things: *simplify* their vocabulary, and speak SLOWLY, CLEARLY and LOUDLY (like when working against Daily Jargon Fatigue).

While practising for a presentation, or just doing your Weekly Speaking Training, give this exercise a try. Imagine you're speaking to a child or an elderly family member, and think how you would explain your pitch or presentation to them in a way they'd under-stand. Read your script all the way through, changing words where necessary and speaking with the required Speech Settings.

This will help you both EDIT and REHEARSE your script, so this one is a double whammy!

3. "Soundtrack"

What's your favourite "pump-up" song? Something by Metallica? 50 Cent? Katy Perry? A.R. Rahman? Tchaikovsky?

Whatever it is, it should be something rousing that gets you motivated and excited; something you might play while working out or running. While *rehearsing*, play that song on your phone, computer, or, better yet, on Bluetooth speakers, and SPEAK OVER THE MUSIC! This will make sure you are LOUD ENOUGH TO BE HEARD, but also allow the *emotion* of the music to infuse your speaking with energy, enthusiasm, or whatever feelings the song stirs up in you.[42]

4. Clapping for emphasis OR clapping to work against "upspeak"

Clapping can be a great sensory and auditory exercise when prac-tising your public speaking, as the noise and the feeling of clapping your hands together on certain words or syllables can help train your brain. This exercise can be used for two purposes:

    a. for non-native English speakers to improve their pronunciation of difficult words, and

    b. for people to work against "high rising terminal" intonation, more popularly known as "uptalk/upspeak" — the phenom-enon of saying statements with a rising inflection at the end, making it sound like a question ("Hi? My name is Will? I'm a speaking coach?" You'll know it when you hear it!).

For a):

If you're an ESL learner who's having trouble with either your Clarity or pronunciation in English, try using this exercise to help you master some of the more difficult sounds.

    i. Choose the word you want to practise.

    ii. Type it into Google.

---

42 Fun fact: Sergio Leone and Ennio Morricone, the director and composer duo behind cinematic masterpieces like *The Good, the Bad and the Ugly* and *Once Upon a Time in the West*, would sometimes compose and record the music for their films *before* they shot the scenes. This was so they could play the music over loudspeakers on set, to have the actors feel the emotion of the score and let it inform their performances. One of my favourite YouTubers, "Nerdwriter," has a beautiful video on the subject called "Why Sergio Leone Played Music on Set." I highly recommend this video, and his whole channel.

iii. Use the Google dictionary and press the 🔊 icon to listen, making sure you know *how many syllables* there are in the word (don't assume you know: my clients are often wrong!) and which is the *stressed* syllable.

iv. Once you know how many syllables, and which is stressed, practise saying the word OUT LOUD, SLOWLY, separating the syllables, and *clapping* your hands on each syllable, with an extra-hard **CLAP** on the stressed syllable. For example, if the word is "personalization," you would say it like this:

ˈperˈ	ˈsoˈ	ˈnaˈ	ˈliˈ	**ˈZAˈ**	ˈtionˈ
clap	*clap*	*clap*	*clap*	***CLAP***	*clap*

Make sure you clap at the same time as you say the syllables! This exercise will help you SLOW DOWN and EMPHASIZE each of them.

For b):

To help you work against upspeak, clap at the *end* of your sentences to make sure your voice is LANDING on the final words rather than rising upwards as if you were asking a question. The clapping action makes it feel as though you are landing hard, which will train you to make the statement in a hard, authoritative way.

So instead of:

"My name is Will?"

Practise saying:

"My name is ˈ**WILL**ˈ! (CLAP!)"

You can try this one out (with your own first name) right now, if you want!

5. "Hold your tongue"

This exercise is super-simple, drama class 101. Stick your tongue out of your mouth, and either hold it between your index finger and thumb, or, if that grosses you out, just keep your tongue out there. Then, read through your entire script, keeping your tongue out or in your fingers, but making sure that you speak SLOWLY, LOUDLY and CLEARLY enough to *still be understood.* Like many of these exercises, you can ask someone to listen and confirm if they understand you, or you can record yourself and watch or listen back.

By isolating your tongue, you train the rest of your mouth muscles to work extra-hard to be understood. This one will feel and sound goofy, but it's amazingly effective!

6. Box with key words

Any type of movement helps us when we need to memorize a script. Studies show that actors who walked around when memorizing lines had 20% better recall than actors who stayed seated while memorizing.[43] I used to swim laps and recite my Shakespeare monologue before auditioning for theatre school, connecting each front-crawl stroke to a word or phrase. For some reason, movement helps memory. Moving while rehearsing can also help raise your energy level, and help you practise connecting your words to your physical expression.

You can recite your text as you jog, lift weights, do yoga, walk the dog, or even wash dishes. Any kind of movement will help you memorize your words.

---

43 Noice, H. & Noice, T. (2001). "Learning dialogue with and without movement." *Memory & Cognition, 29,* 820-827. 10.3758/BF03196411

Boxing, however, has an even greater benefit, in that you can attach a PUNCH to a KEY WORD, which will train you to emphasize those words with power and precision.

First, get in a boxing stance: stand up, place your left foot ahead of your right foot (or vice versa, if you're left-handed), ball your hands into fists and get them up by your chin, with your elbows pointing down. To begin with, throw only jabs (lead hand punches) and straight crosses (rear hand punches) — what boxers call "the one and the two" — to keep things simple. Read through your script, *punching* on the *key words*. Each punch should be in unison with a key word, like the clapping exercise from earlier. Rhythm is important!

Here's an example. If your script says:

"Our incredible product is five times faster than current solutions."

then you would **punch the air** on the following **bolded** and ***italicized words***:

"Our ***incredible product*** is ***five times faster*** than **current** solutions."

This one is also great for getting your energy levels up, and making you feel more powerful!

7. Imitate a public speaking hero

Think of your favourite public speaker, comedian, politician, late-night host, podcaster, TV personality, or even an old teacher or mentor who you admire. What makes them so *engaging*, vocally and physically? Can you identify their Speech Settings, funny patterns, vocal habits, or any catchphrases they have?

Doing the best you can, read through your script doing an

imitation of someone you love listening to, in the way you imagine they would do it.

This is a great way to show yourself how different your voice can sound, as well as to shake things up and have fun. Don't worry about being accurate, just enjoy the mimicry!

8. "Image" key words

We work on *key words* a lot in OutLoud coaching sessions. In fact, I often say if there's only one piece of speaking advice I could give, it would be: "Emphasize your key words."

The human brain can't possibly take in and remember *all* the information you give it — it's going to filter out what doesn't seem important and look for what does. Knowing this, you can help your audience by *highlighting* the *key words* (the info you really want them to hear and remember) not just by emphasizing them vocally and physically, but also by being more *emotionally connected* to what you're saying.

Now, what does that actually mean — to be "emotionally connected"?

At theatre school, and even in many rehearsal rooms, directors will have you close your eyes and visualize certain parts of your script. For example, if your character says, "We used to live in a little apartment on 21st Street," the director might ask you to close your eyes and think of the word "apartment."

What do you see? What colour are the walls? What can be seen out the windows? What are the sounds inside and outside the apartment? What's the neighbourhood like? What are the smells inside the kitchen? What does the furniture feel like? Is it clean? Dirty? Fancy? Simple? What is the feeling inside the home? Love? Tension? Fear?

You can also do this as a real memory visualization, not just as a hypothetical imagination exercise. For example:

What was your earliest memory of your home? Was it an apartment or a house? Which was your favourite room? Your least favourite? What kinds of sounds, smells and feelings did this apartment or house have? What was the building like? Was it friendly, or scary?

This meditation on the simple word "apartment" means that when the actor finally says the word during a performance, it's loaded with all the sense memory or imagination that came up during the meditation. The audience, even though they don't know it, will *feel* the weight and specificity of these words, and if the actor has done their job, the audience will be able to visualize their own version of what these words mean. And a lot of that work is done in rehearsal through techniques like this *imaging exercise.*

The reason we only use this technique on key words is because it's a waste of time to "image" words like "going" or "the" or "of," because they're not important for the audience to hear, remember and visualize. Phrases like "life-saving medicine," "thousands of happy customers" or "$30 billion in revenue" ARE very important, however, so these are the ones we want to practise visualizing.

To do this exercise, choose one or two of your MOST IMPORT-ANT KEY WORDS and PHRASES from your script, close your eyes, and picture everything you can related to that word/phrase. If your word was "hospital," for example, you could visualize it through:

- Word association: sick, nurses, machines, death, sad, families
- Sense memory: sounds (beeping, crying), smells (cleaning products), sensations (cold, hard chairs), etc.

- People you associate with the word: "my grandpa at the end of his life," "my childhood friend who was sick," "my wife, who's a doctor," etc.
- Memories: e.g., "when I was a kid I stepped on a nail and had to be rushed to the emergency room, my sister was there and my mum was holding my hand"
- TV shows or movies: e.g., *Grey's Anatomy, ER, Scrubs, John Q.,* etc.

Once you've thought along these lines for a few minutes, open your eyes and read JUST *the sentence that contains the word you've been "imaging."* Try to say it with all the images in your mind so that the word has weight to it.

This "key word imaging" exercise is useful whenever you have new material to learn, or you're feeling like you've said your script so many times it's losing its meaning. The final benefit of imaging is that it stirs up emotions in you by helping you remember things from your past related to family and childhood, and this is a beautiful state of mood to speak from.

9. The "apple technique"

This is one of my favourites — it's so easy and fun to do. Grab an apple and eat it as you read through your script. For some reason, this will make you more relaxed, funny, expressive, and yet conversational as you speak. For reference, watch the darkly comedic scene from *300* with Gerard Butler as he eats an apple while killing wounded enemy soldiers, or the *Seinfeld* episode "The Phone Message," where George is convinced he sounds more confident and sexy when talking to women on the phone if he eats an apple.

Just trust me on this one: it works, and it also allows you to have a snack and work on your skills at the same time!

10. "Italian" run-through

No disrespect to my Italian people out there, but this is what North American actors call it when they read through or rehearse their lines at DOUBLE SPEED. I guess they think that Italians speak at a rapid-fire pace, which, of course, depends on where in Italy you're from or what your personality type is. In any case, before we get too into the weeds on this or offend anyone further, let's just look at the exercise.

Once you've memorized your text (this can be done by using the *movement helps memory* principle mentioned earlier, or whatever memorization technique works for you), say it *as fast as you can* while still being *clear*. This will force your brain to prepare you for the next sentence faster than usual, and allow you to get several practice runs in during a short time. This is especially helpful if you're about to go on stage or on camera.

So, those are the TOP TEN exercises. I have used and taught every single one of them, and I hope you trust me that, however silly or useless they may seem to you, they really do work. With these, you'll never get bored of rehearsing again, and the results onstage or on camera from all the preparation you've done will be evident to everyone. Don't be surprised if you start getting compliments on your talks very soon after starting to incorporate these exercises into your rehearsal!

Now, let's recap Act 5: Automation, or the steps to becoming your own coach:

SUMMARY

- James Clear, author of *Atomic Habits*, says: "You don't rise to the level of your goals; you fall to the level of your systems." Habits are more important than goals.
- The French word for rehearsal is *répétition*, indicating that in order to practise a performance properly, you need to do it many times, over and over.
- Practice makes perfect, as the saying goes, but practice must be done the right way, so that poor technique does not become ingrained.
- Daily Jargon Fatigue (DJF) is the phenomenon of saying common expressions and words in a quick, low mumble. This is caused by "the curse of knowledge," and the human instinct to be lazy and shorten words.
- Counter DJF by highlighting the words that are potentially vulnerable to it, saying them exaggeratedly SLOWLY, LOUDLY and CLEARLY.
- Exaggerate in rehearsal (especially when working against your habits) so that you can be normal on the day you deliver your presentation or pitch.
- Rehearsal variations are important: we need to rehearse our talk many times, but if we do it the same way each time it can get monotonous and robotic.

In the next and final section of this book, I'm going to show you how to put together a TRAINING PROGRAM with all of these exercises, plus more standard ones like stretching, breathing, or workouts, as well as how to stay motivated and on track with this routine.

This is the last part of our journey, so let's finish strong!

YOUR 30-DAY OUTLOUD TRAINING PROGRAM

This is it: the moment when we put all this anecdotal, emotional, pseudo-scientific and chaotic theory into cold, hard practice, so we can see what happens when we actually work at our craft.

This is the gym, the dojo, the studio, the drawing board. Here is where we practise our craft, again and again, until something new emerges. And then, we keep working! Transforming your speaking skills, like every worthwhile pursuit, never ends. As with meditation, cooking, yoga, guitar, learning a language, or therapy, there's no such thing as perfect or finished. We keep working on our speaking skills until the day we die, because there's always more to know and new ways to hear and be heard even better.

But even though you'll never be perfect, you can still transform your speaking skills in a relatively short period — let's say 30 days.

In this chapter I'm going to give you a training program that will sketch out your plan for the next 30 days, which you'll be able to follow no matter how busy you say you are and transform not only your speaking skills, but also how you feel in mind and body. Using all the principles, techniques and exercises we've learned, we're going to make sure that you are improving your craft every day and increasing your wellbeing as a result!

In *Atomic Habits* (in my opinion, the Bible of good habit formation), James Clear talks about the power of Tiny "Gains". The idea is that, through compounding, if you get one percent better at something every day for a year, by the end of that year you'll be 38 times better at that thing. Conversely, if you get one percent worse every day over the same period, you'll go down to almost zero.

To sum up, if you put in a bit of effort every day, you'll be unrecognizable in a year's time — in a good way. However, if you go a year *without* practising, you'll be unrecognizable in a bad way. I can't tell you how many people came to me after a year of COVID lockdowns feeling like they'd lost all their public speaking confidence. On the flip side, when former clients contact me a year after doing one of my programs and sticking with the work, they report huge advances in their business or career, and more confidence than ever.

With Clear's Tiny Gains in mind, we want to create a schedule that is:

- immediately effective,
- doable,
- fun,
- varied,
- compounding, and
- sticky (as in, you'll stick to it. I didn't know what other adjective to use).

Nothing too time-consuming or ambitious will work, and nobody wants to do training that bores them. You want to see results right away, and you need assurance of long-term success. I believe the following schedule can be done by almost anyone, regardless of how busy they are. And the best part is, it's fun and makes you feel good!

But first, here's a list of exercises that you can use *alongside* the Top Ten Speaking Exercises to help you improve your speaking skills, confidence, and wellbeing. For some of these, it will be your choice when or whether to use them:

- yoga
- mindfulness meditation (guided)
- mindfulness meditation (silent or with music)
- working on your Problem>Solution>Prize statement from Act 2: Articulation
- filming your 60-second videos from Act 3: Action and posting them online
- reading out loud
- reading fiction
- listening to audio books
- reading non-fiction works about storytelling, public speaking, communication, leadership, and psychology
- singing
- watching Netflix with an eye on the STORY and the ACTING
- watching documentaries or YouTube videos and noticing the speakers' Speech Settings
- dancing
- running, boxing, swimming, or doing any cardio exercise
- listening to long-form podcasts

We can include all of these in our public speaking, communication, and storytelling program because when you work on your:

- voice,
- body,

- mind,
- mental health,
- personal awareness, and
- understanding of art, story, fiction, performance, conversation, etc.,

you are also working on your speaking skills!

So, let's get into it! What follows is a very basic set of activities to do over 30 days, which will take you no more than 15 minutes a day. In my opinion, most of the meditations and warm-ups are best done in the morning, but you can do them whenever you like: after lunch, before bed, or whenever you have 10 free minutes between the kids, work, and everything else.

I've broken up the 30 days into the five acts of the OutLoud Method. Each section will build on the previous one, just like we do in our courses.

THE 30-DAY OUTLOUD TRAINING PROGRAM

Act 1: Awareness

- **Day 1**: guided mindfulness meditation for 10 minutes in the morning. Five minutes of yoga in the afternoon.
- **Day 2**: OutLoud Warm-Up (OLWU) for 5 minutes before work or a big meeting. Ten minutes of yoga sometime in the afternoon, during a work break.
- **Day 3**: OLWU for 5 minutes in the morning. Watch 10 minutes of a Speaking Hero (YouTuber, podcaster, etc.) and take note of their Speech Settings ("Volume = 7," "Pace = 2," etc.).
- **Day 4**: OLWU for 5 minutes, right before you spend 10

minutes making a 60-second video introducing yourself or giving your elevator pitch.

- **Day 5**: any guided mindfulness meditation in the morning for 5 minutes.[44] Spend 10 minutes watching a video of you introducing yourself or giving your elevator pitch, and take notes on your Speech Settings.

- **Day 6**: yoga for 15 minutes —turn off your brain and get into your body! Afterwards, eat something or drink coffee, or do something you find pleasurable as a reward. You can use this reward system every day if you like, but I'll remind you through this program!

Act 2: Articulation

- **Day 7**: OLWU in the morning for 5 minutes. Ten minutes brainstorming your Problem>Solution>Prize (P>S>P) statement from Act 2: Articulation. (*Who do you help with what problem and why? What's your solution and how does it work? What benefit do they get from working with you?*)

- **Day 8**: OutLoud's guided meditation on "Your Story,"[45] whenever you like, for 10 minutes. Work on your P>S>P statement for 5 minutes.

- **Day 9**: OLWU in the morning for 5 minutes, starting to experiment with making it your own: changing tongue twisters, doing different stretches, feeling what your body needs. Cardio for at least 10 minutes while listening to a good podcast, after work or during a break.

---

44 I recommend the Great Meditation channel on YouTube. They post awesome 10-minute meditations every day.

45 Greenblatt, W. (2021, August 30). "Monday Morning Meditation – Your Story." YouTube. https://www.youtube.com/watch?v=qgtPm950Rmw&t=51s.

- **Day 10**: silent meditation for 5 minutes in the morning. Practise reading your P>S>P statement out loud (editing if necessary) for 10 minutes.
- **Day 11**: 155 minutes of writing work, answering the following questions:

1. *Why did you start your current business or career?*
2. *Was there a "lightbulb moment"? Describe it in detail.*
3. *How does your work have a positive impact on the world?*
4. *What are some things you used to think or believe that have changed because of the work you do now?*
5. *Why do you think your personality fits the work you do?*
6. *What's the lowest professional moment you've had?*
7. *What's the best professional moment you've had?*
8. *Why do you get up every day to do this work?*

Reward yourself at the end of this writing exercise!
- **Day 12**: yoga for 10 minutes in the morning. Spend 5 minutes finalizing your P>S>P statement before the end of the work day, and save it as an *editable document* so you can use it whenever you need to (for writing presentations, copy for your website, sending someone your bio, etc.).

Act 3: Action

- **Day 13**: OLWU for 5 minutes. *Immediately afterwards*, record yourself reading your P>S>P statement, or any text (30-60 seconds' worth), using "Speaking Exercise #1: Exaggerate a Speech Setting" (Volume at a 9 if you usually speak softly, Pace at a 2 if you speak fast, etc.).
- **Day 14**: Video Studio Self-Assessment for 15 minutes. How

is your lighting? How does your audio sound in your videos? How's the background? Sound insulation? Do you need to buy anything to make yourself look and sound better online or on video? Make a list. Refer to the section in Act 3: Action, "What equipment do I need?" to remind yourself what to do to optimize your video set-up.

- **Day 15**: OLWU for 5 minutes. *Immediately afterwards*, record yourself reading your P>S>P statement or any text, using your new video set-up as your "set" and doing 10 minutes' worth of recording and watching back.

- **Day 16**: spend 15 minutes seeking opportunities to speak. Volunteer yourself to your manager for the next sales pre- sentation; look on LinkedIn for events you'd be qualified for, and then DM the event manager; create your own free webi- nar on Eventbrite; give a toast at a birthday party. Whatever it is, take 15 minutes to look into creating an extra public speaking gig for yourself. Reward yourself when done by petting your dog, playing your favourite mobile game, or eating something sweet!

- **Day 17**: OLWU for 5 minutes. *Immediately afterwards*, record yourself reading for 5 minutes, using "Speaking Exercise #3: Soundtrack." Finally, choose a time and day to record and post your WEEKLY VIDEO, and put it in your online or personal calendar (and do it every week, starting from now!).

- **Day 18**: for 15 minutes, try to memorize several lines of text. It could be a chunk of an upcoming presentation, your ele- vator pitch, your favourite monologue from a movie, or a paragraph of a book you love. Whatever it is, use "Speaking Exercise #6: Boxing on Key Words" to help you memorize, emphasize and get the blood flowing! If you get stuck, refer to the text. When the 15 minutes are up, recite it from memory as best you can!

Act 4: Alignment

- **Day 19**: guided meditation for 10 minutes in the morning on some sort of "life's purpose" topic (choose something from Great Meditation on YouTube; I recommend a video titled "Higher Self"). Record a 60-second video on the topic "My *ikigai*." Spend 5 minutes to get a take you feel good about, but no more! Afterwards, do something you like as a reward.
- **Day 20**: OLWU for 5 minutes in the morning, experimenting and using whatever exercises you need to wake yourself up or feel good — make it your own! Complete the following writing exercise:

   "I want to seem _____ . But I'm terrified I come across as _____ . I think this is because _____ ."

   Write as much as you can or want to in 10 minutes.
- **Day 21**: silent meditation for 5 minutes in the morning. *Immediately afterwards*, spend 10 minutes journaling, writing down any negative or positive thoughts about yourself that came up during your meditation (e.g., "I'm so stupid, I forgot to take the garbage out last night," or "I'm proud of myself for doing this").
- **Day 22**: yoga for 10 minutes in the morning. For 5 minutes while at work, do "Speaking Exercise #7: Imaging" for some of the key words you use every day.
- **Day 23**: Watch your "My *ikigai*" video from Day 19, and re-record it to see if you can do it better — more *authentic,*

enthusiastic, passionate, etc. — in terms of both the content and the delivery. Do a quick 60-second warm-up if you need to, and then record. No more than 15 minutes on all of this. Reward after!

- **Day 24**: Pick a Speaking Hero and watch their content. See if you can identify what makes them so engaging, paying attention to Speech Settings and Alignment.

Act 5: Automation

- **Day 25**: rehearsal = *répétition*. Spend 15 minutes working on some text, using whatever exercises you like, doing it over and over.

- **Day 26**: OLWU for 5 minutes. Immediately afterwards, record a 60-second video — this is the very first that you will put out on social media, YouTube, or your company's website. (Explain what kind of videos you want to be making, for whom, and the P>S>P of your videos.) At the end of the video, and in your caption, tell your audience that you will be posting WEEKLY videos (this will make you accountable).

    Take at least 10 minutes or longer on this today, as this one's important! After you're done, reward yourself with a chocolate, a coffee, or whatever will make you feel good.

- **Day 27**: choose a time to do "OutLoud work," i.e., something for your speaking skills, every day. (Remember, this can include meditation, working out, yoga, reading, any one of the Top Ten Speaking Exercises, etc. — which are all good things to do every day.) Put a 15-minute block in your calendar, and in your calendar notes write a list of possible exercises you could do. Make it repeat daily at the same time. But take weekends off!

- **Day 28**: at the time you chose on Day 27, do your own version of a 15-minute OutLoud workout, using whatever exercises you like. Reward yourself at the end .
- **Day 29**: same as above. Habits: behaviour, reward!
- **Day 30**: RECORD AND POST A VIDEO about the last 30 days, titled "My 30-Day Public Speaking Transformation," about your experience. Notice all the amazing confidence and clarity you're speaking with, and the positive encouragement you get from your friends, family and followers. Tag me @willgreenblatt, and I'll review it for free and give you free feedback and congratulations!

THE END!

That's it! Thirty days of positive habit formation, seeing what works for you, probably missing some days, learning how that feels, getting back on the horse, and all the while improving by 1% each time. If you complete even a portion of this program, I guarantee you will feel the results in your confidence, clarity, and wellbeing.

So, where do you go from here? There's only one direction you will go if you follow this 30-day program, and begin to absorb the message of this book: towards a *transformation of your speaking skills*. You can become a brilliant, engaging public speaker and leader, deliver powerful presentations, inspire audiences, and change lives. The only direction you will go is up — perhaps, one day, to the very top of your profession. I can't wait to hear from you when you do!

CONCLUSION:

OUR STORIES ARE STILL BEING WRITTEN

I've come a hell of a long way to be writing this book, and having you read it. I've come from being terrified, depressed, anxious, self-loathing and completely purposeless to being the founder of a company that allows me to help thousands of people with their speaking skills, which in turn helps them lead their lives with more confidence and purpose. No matter how much money I make, that will always be the biggest prize, as it is for almost every passionate entrepreneur or businessperson I know. Helping others, having fun, getting paid and being recognized for it — this is the *ikigai* that drives us.

I believe you can do this for yourself, too. Through the power of words, you can change the way you communicate, the way you talk to yourself, the stories you tell, and ultimately transform your life into one of happiness, service, wealth, and recognition.

To get there, however, reading this book is not enough (obviously). You must put the work in and commit to continuing the work for the rest of your life. The joy must be in the process of discovering new ways to communicate, or motivate others, or teach, or inspire, or lead.

If you can fall in love with this work, like I have, you'll never be bored by a conversation again, because you can always learn something from the person who's talking to you. You'll find yourself fascinated by listening to the most painfully dull presentations, because you'll have a framework for judging them and thinking of how you could help the speaker. And eventually, you'll be able to pass this passion on to others in your company, field, or family, and watch the positive ripple effects spread.

Here's how you can continue this work if you've decided that you want to be a powerful speaker as part of your career:

- Keep your training program going! Commit to 15 minutes a day, or at least every other day. Try to never take two days off in a row. Remember: yoga, meditation, cardio, singing, dancing, reading — it all counts!
- Post 60-second videos talking about your area of expertise WEEKLY (ideally more) on social media (recommended format at time of writing: IG Reels, YouTube Shorts, TikTok, LinkedIn).
- Follow me on social media (search for "Will Greenblatt" or "OutLoud Speakers School"), where I post daily speaking tips.
- Email my company at info@outloudnow.com to find out how I can help you or your team with your public speaking skills.
- Book me for an event to come talk to your group!

I hope you enjoyed reading this book, and that it inspired you and gave you some tools to start your own journey of transformation. If it did, please consider recommending it to a friend, or leaving a review on Amazon, GoodReads or Google Books. It would really help me out.

I'll end with a quote from Brené Brown:

> *"One day you'll tell your story, and it will*
> *be someone else's survival guide."*

You have so much to share with the world. Start sharing it, and keep sharing it — when it's all said and done, you'll be so glad you did.

www.ingramcontent.com/pod-product-compliance
Lightning Source LLC
Chambersburg PA
CBHW031528120626
46545CB00005B/2046